"It's half-time; the team are losing, dispirited and feeling all is lost. Suddenly into the dressing room walk Gavin and Anne Calver. They coach, they yell, they inspire – they teach. When the team hit the pitch at the start of the second half everybody can see that something has changed. Game Changers is a book for the church in our times".

Rob Parsons OBE, Chairman, Care for the Family

"This book reminds us that we have the ability to change the game; not only for us, but also for those we may never even get to know this side of heaven. Our generous God continues to invite us to come so the question is not, "will He invite, but rather will we accept His invitation?"

Christy Wimber, international speaker and Senior Pastor at Yorba Linda Vineyard

"This book has inspired me to rediscover my passion for making a difference. It's honest and practical, and set my mind and heart buzzing about what I can do, however small, that will help build God's kingdom."

Abby Guinness, Event Director, Spring Harvest

"This book is brilliant! It's packed full of inspirational spirit filled stories and practical advice for anyone who seriously wants to engage in the joy and challenges of mission."

Rev Virginia Luckett, Director UK Churches Team, Tearfund and Associate Vicar, All Saints Isleworth

D0513243

Also by Gavin and Anne Calver:
Disappointed with Jesus?
Lazy, Antisocial and Selfish?
Stumbling Blocks
12 Disciples (Anne Calver and Andy Flannagan)
On the Front Line (Gavin and Clive Calver)

Evangelical Alliance

The Evangelical Alliance is the largest and oldest body representing the UK's two million evangelical Christians. The Alliance is passionate about making Jesus known in every sphere of society. That's why for nearly 170 years, it has been bringing Christians together and helping them listen to, and be heard by, the government, media and society. The Alliance works towards two main goals: for the Church to be united in mission, and confident and effective in voice. Will you join us?

www.eauk.org/join

GAME
CHANGERS

ENCOUNTERING GOD
AND CHANGING THE WORLD

Gavin & Anne Calver

MONARCH
BOOKS

Oxford, UK, and Grand Rapids, USA

Text copyright © 2016 Gavin and Anne Calver
This edition copyright © 2016 Lion Hudson

The right of Gavin and Anne Calver to be identified as the authors of this work has been asserted by them in accordance with the Copyright, Designs and Patents Act 1988.

All rights reserved. No part of this publication may be reproduced or transmitted in any form or by any means, electronic or mechanical, including photocopy, recording, or any information storage and retrieval system, without permission in writing from the publisher.

Published by Monarch Books (an imprint of Lion Hudson plc)
Wilkinson House, Jordan Hill Road, Oxford OX2 8DR, England
Email: monarch@lionhudson.com www.lionhudson.com/monarch
and by Elevation (an imprint of the Memralife Group)
Memralife Group, 14 Horsted Square, Uckfield, East Sussex TN22 1QG
Tel: +44 (0)1825 746530; Fax +44 (0)1825 748899;
www.elevationmusic.com

ISBN 978 0 85721 724 0
e-ISBN 978 0 85721 725 7

First edition 2016

Acknowledgments
Unless stated otherwise, Scripture quotations taken from the Holy Bible, New International Version Anglicised. Copyright © 1979, 1984, 2011 Biblica, formerly International Bible Society. Used by permission of Hodder & Stoughton Ltd, an Hachette UK company. All rights reserved. "NIV" is a registered trademark of Biblica. UK trademark number 1448790. Scripture quotations marked NLT are taken from the Holy Bible, New Living Translation, copyright © 1996, 2004, 2007 by Tyndale House Foundation. Used by permission of Tyndale House Publishers, Inc., Carol Stream, Illinois 60188. All rights reserved.
Extracts pp. 27, 48, 123 taken from *Straight to the Heart of Moses* by Phil Moore, copyright © 2011 Phil Moore. Used by permission.
Extract p. 109 taken from "Two Rows by the Sea" by The Bible Society of Egypt, copyright © 2015 The Bible Society of Egypt. Used by permission.
Extract p. 129 taken from "The Butterfly Song" by Brian M. Howard, copyright © 1974, 2002 Mission Hills Music www.ButterflySong.com. All rights reserved. Used by permission.
Extracts p. 243 taken from "Great Is Thy Faithfulness" by Thomas O. Chisholm © Hope Publishing Company. Used by permission; and "Footprints in the Sand" by Mary Stevenson, copyright © Mary Stevenson. Used by permission.
"A Prayer for Hope" p. 244 taken from www.prayers-for-special-help.com. Used by permission.

A catalogue record for this book is available from the British Library
Printed and bound in the UK, February 2016, LH36

We have loved writing this book and have felt hugely challenged by the idea of being game changers. We long to see a real move of God in this land and are desperate to play our part in this. We are grateful for many friends who've helped us on this journey, especially those who read earlier manuscripts and were so helpful in their feedback. We are massively thankful to the Spring Harvest team for the opportunity to write the 2016 theme book, and to the folks there for all their help and support.

This is not the full story of Moses; it's the story of a number of pivotal moments in his life and that of the Israelites that hold great relevance today. We're not telling the story of Israel in the wilderness, but the transformation in Moses that began at the burning bush and ended with Joshua taking the Promised Land.

As co-authors, we have both contributed to every chapter. When the story in the chapter ends, the writer may well change, but be assured that every sentence has been agreed together.

Enjoy the ride!

Contents

Foreword

The Church of Jesus Christ is the most exciting, vibrant and life changing community on earth – at least it is supposed to be. If we have lost those traits, then we had best rediscover them. The world around us changes rapidly and a Church that is unable to adapt and roll with the punches will soon wither and die. A look at our history as the People of God shows us many things that we would do well to remember.

Firstly, that we are at our best when we are brave. We are called to celebrate the common good, challenge the culture of our day, stand up for what is right, speak with humble confidence, serve with unconditional determination and proclaim the Good News of Jesus' life, death, burial, and resurrection with tenacity and passion. Martyn Lloyd-Jones once said that the Church is most effective when she is most different from the world, even if the world hates her for a while.

Secondly, we are at our weakest when we become nothing more than a pale imitation of the world around us. Our society needs more than a nice Church; it needs a bold, courageous and faithful Church.

Game Changers reminds us that we each have a part to play. It challenges us to rediscover the things that really matter. It forces us to think about the principles that shape our lives as Christians. It calls for a clearer vision of God, a deeper experience of His Spirit, and a stronger commitment to His cause. As you read it, you will begin to feel something stirring in your soul. I hope that you will be unsettled by the book. I am praying that you will be disconcerted by it, and that you will yearn for a fresh outbreaking of God's Holy Spirit in our society. I am praying that you will yearn for God to do something fresh and utterly transforming in our day.

Game Changers is not about trying to make you into a hero. The heart of this book is that you might see that the only hero in the Christian story is God Himself and that our lives are lived most fully and most vibrantly when we are reflecting His purposes into the world around us. A game changer doesn't need to be a millionaire or a politician or a mega-celebrity. You can be a game changer as an ordinary man, woman, boy or girl.

I love being a Christian, and I love being part of the Church, but I also get really frustrated with myself and with the Church. We so often settle for the mediocre and sell ourselves short. When we catch a glimpse of what God wants to do through us, however, everything changes! We become bold, courageous, determined and exciting. Above all we become ALIVE.

Game Changers is more than a book. It is a prophetic call to re-discover the amazing purposes of God. I have read this material many times. I will preach it, teach it and, by God's grace, I will seek to live it. I've watched the impact it has had on one family – Anne and Gavin Calver and their children. I've seen God leading them into new risks, new challenges and new seasons. Imagine what would happen if God did that with every person who read this; if we took our eyes off all the things that we think we cannot do and focussed on what we know God can do. Imagine if the Church was a community of people who knew that God had changed the game for them and were willing to do anything that was good and right so that He could change the game for others. The Church of Jesus was once known as those who had turned the world upside down. May our day and our generation see us become known as that again.

Lord, do it in me and do it in others. Light the fire, Lord, change the game.

Malcolm Duncan

Introduction

"The future is not something we enter. The future is something we create."

LEONARD SWEET

A NEW KIND OF LANDSCAPE

We were both born in 1979, which, incidentally, was also the year that Spring Harvest began. For the UK church an awful lot has changed in the time since. Back then the idea of widespread and affordable personal computers would have been like something from a sci-fi film. Phone boxes were the way to communicate on the move, yet, if you see one now, it stands as a memorial to a bygone era. Coffee was a basic item for drinking at home – not a luxury and trendy café option costing the same as a pint of beer. Everything has sped up and we now find ourselves in a world of tablets and smartphones, where the previously unthinkable internet is all that generations of teenagers have ever known. We find ourselves living in the middle of a cultural revolution.

This time, though, it's change like never before, for we are living in the "Digital Revolution". In short this is "the advancement of technology from analog electronic and mechanical devices to the digital technology available today. The era started during the 1980s and is ongoing. The Digital Revolution also marks the beginning of the Information Era."[1] This time is often referred to as **the third industrial revolution**. All of this has had a profound impact on church.

As a body of people we have been far from immune from all that is going on.

As a direct result we are working with a different type of person. The theologian Leonard Sweet describes this new world as a TGIF world; a rising generation whose social interactions and medium of choice are built around Twitter, Google, iPhones and Facebook. He articulates it this way: "If the unit of the premodern world was the family, and the unit of the Gutenberg world was the individual, the unit of the TGIF world is the network. At its best, this means a rediscovery of our being-in-common, the sense of the village square or town commons."[2] Within this context we need to fight for community in an increasingly "virtual" world. This doesn't mean genuine relationships can't be built and maintained virtually; however, it does require that we don't simply have a virtual existence and that we also engage face to face. There are many other sociological changes going on around us and to be truthful you can never understand a revolution fully when you're living in the middle of it.

THE PLACE OF CHRISTIANITY?

In our new-found world it can so often feel like Christianity is marginalized. This has not always been the case. For many hundreds of years, the church in Britain was the very epicentre of the community. Every town and village had a church and a school as two basic necessities for any community. There was real social capital and gravitas to be gained from being part of a local church too. Whether we like it or not the church does not hold this position anymore. The school remains, but often the church building is now used for selling carpets or as an art deco wine bar instead. Where these buildings are in operation still you'll often find a congregation smaller than the number of people needed for a football team.

In June 2015, *Premier Christianity* magazine published some research from the Pew Research Center claiming that, at the going rate of decline, by the year 2050 Christianity will lose its place as the majority religion in Britain.[3] Clearly things are not going well and we need to see real change in this land. However, spirituality is not seen as in any way irrelevant. It is considered central to one's humanity and is massively popular within our culture. There is seemingly a growing spiritual hunger within our society and yet an increasing diffidence towards Christianity. Anything seen as mystical is often pursued whilst the spirituality of the church is not even considered as it is so often perceived as outdated, irrelevant, and past it. The comedian Frank Skinner puts it this way in his autobiography: "In a society where all manner of once smirked upon behavior like wearing crystals and Feng Shui has become acceptable, **only Christian belief can definitely guarantee you the label 'weird'**."[4]

Such a label may be perplexing when we consider Britain's Christian heritage. When did Christianity become a "weird" religion? What was once seen as true is now false; what many once considered bizarre is now normal. This has all happened in a relatively short space of time. That in itself gives us hope that a reversal of current trends might prove equally rapid.

There has also been a dramatic rise in credibility, acceptance, and indeed promotion of militant atheism. Spearheaded by Richard Dawkins, increasingly many famous voices have added their weight to the atheist camp. Within our society there is also **an intellectual bias towards atheism**. It is often seen as intellectually superior, whilst in order to be a Christian you can just leave your brain at the door.

Staunch atheist Stephen Fry was asked by Irish journalist Gay Byrne what he would say to God at the pearly gates if it turned out it was all true his answer was arresting. Part of his response was to say, "Why should I respect a capricious, mean-minded, stupid God who creates a world that is so full of injustice and pain. That's what I would say."[5] Such views are growing and Fry's comments were well received by the secularists and responded to with an often ludicrous sense of insecurity from Christians. Increasingly our faith can feel marginalized.

However **we don't believe in the God that Fry and many others describe in such ways either!** What they are drawing out is a mistaken view of who He is. Fry's comment does speak to difficult questions surrounding suffering that we all grapple with. As Christians, however, our view of God is more complex than that of the "capricious, mean-minded" one that Fry describes. Where does Jesus figure into his argument? What of the God of compassion, who sacrificed His own Son for the betterment of humanity? And we cannot discount the role of human free will that is exercised, for good and for evil, in the world. Our triune God cannot be reduced to a "stupid", pain-loving deity. With respect to Fry he is an atheist and his views on a God he doesn't believe exists are therefore shallow in places.

In our current context it is not all bad news. Many are still seeking God in the midst of cultural confusion. In his book *Revolution*, Russell Brand seeks to engage with a generation that he believes to be disenfranchised in postmodern Britain. He writes with long words and passion and his book is highly engaging throughout, though in truth not all of his conclusions are entirely thought through. Nonetheless many of his views on God are profound. We were particularly moved by his view that "All desires are the inappropriate substitute for the desire to be at one with God."[6] You don't need to know a lot about Brand to know that he is fairly experienced when it comes to indulging in desires that are, shall we say, "inappropriate". However, as he says in the book, these have all proved to be empty and fruitless once the buzz wears off. It is fun in the moment but none of this brings any sense of fulfilment, meaning or hope in the long term. The world tells us to pursue hedonism but in the end, when the party is over, what are you left with? A headache the next morning and an emptiness in the soul.

We are not the first people to face a difficult landscape. The central biblical character in this book, Moses, didn't have it all easy either. The great theologian Alec Motyer points out that in his context he faced "a task of unparalleled magnitude and difficulty in which he would have to face demands never experienced before".[7] We all face deep cultural challenges and opposition in our own time and have to cling on to God and take on the world in His name. Regardless of what's going on around us, following Jesus remains the only way to know what it is to live. No matter what the cultural climate you can only fully live once you've met the Author of Life. **Truth is not relative to the environment that it finds itself in**, but it does need to be clung onto whilst the waves of an indifferent society seek to drag us under!

STEP UP CHURCH

So we can be in little doubt that we find ourselves living in interesting times. There is a growing temptation for us to fit in with the society of which we are a part. There's this word so many love to use as if it's the hallmark of a perfect society: we need to be "inclusive". Yet today this word seems to mean that you can't have a view on anything or any opinions. We Christians are instead called to be tolerant. Tolerance means learning to live in harmony alongside those that disagree with us – not all having to sign up to the same "McDonaldized" ideologies on everything. Looking to Jesus in His time, He was the most inclusive figure in human history, yet He carried the most exclusive message if you were to follow Him. Just look at the Greeks in John 12. They wanted to "see" Jesus, not fully live for Him with everything they had. As such this is not enough. If you want to follow Jesus then it needs to be all in!

The church was never intended to fit in with no differentiation between her and the society she inhabits. We are not called to become bland magnolia wallpaper on the bare walls of the world, but instead to stand out within it as vibrant, colourful and distinct. **Christians should be influencers, not the influenced**. We want to be bringing others along with us as opposed to being drawn along with them. We should be following the way of Christ, which will often be directly counter to the cultural norm.

In the Sermon on the Mount, this is explained clearly when we are called as a body of Christians to be "salt and light" in the world. The famous German theologian Dietrich Bonhoeffer wrote about what this truly means in his wonderful book *The Cost of Discipleship*:

> Up to now we must have had the impression that the blessed ones were too good for this world, and only

fit to live in heaven. But now Jesus calls them the salt
of the earth – salt, the most indispensable necessity
of life. The disciples, that is to say, are the highest
good, the supreme value which the earth possesses,
for without them it cannot live.[8]

We are here to flavour the world and bring about difference within it. We must be salt that hasn't lost its flavour and light that hasn't run out of battery! We can be confident too that however hard it is to be distinct Jesus is with us. In those places where it feels impossible, there He is. In those times we feel most marginalized, He stands with us. In those moments of our greatest victories, there too is He. After all, the Bible repeats the command "do not be afraid", and then, arguably, the most common promise in Scripture that God makes to His people is "I am with you." With these two realities in place nothing should be impossible!

We must be a church on a mission in a world that desperately needs to see and hear the love of God. If we are ever a club for ourselves then we have missed the point. For us to be church we need to be in mission. Alan Hirsch puts it like this: "When the church is in mission, it is the true church... The mission of God flows directly through every believer and every community of faith that adheres to Jesus. To obstruct this is to block God's purposes in and through his people."[9] We must be a church on a mission seeking to make a huge impact in our world, desperately doing all we can to make a difference and bring about real change. After all, it was the former Archbishop of Canterbury William Temple who said that **"the church is the only institution on earth designed entirely for the benefit of its non-members"**. That kind of church is one on a mission.

GAME CHANGERS

The time has come to see cultural transformation for Christ in this land. We want to see a changing of the spiritual climate, an uprising of the church, a transformation of the UK. In short we want to see Britain turned inside out, upside down, and back to front for Christ.

It's time for a bunch of game changers to rise up and take their place standing strong for Christ. The UK church has been lacking confidence in the gospel for too long. The time has come for us not to be ashamed of "whose" we are. Postmodernity says that the most important thing is who you are. It's as if the entire world revolves around us in this individualistic culture we inhabit. In truth, it's far more important *whose* you are as opposed to *who* you are. Whose are we? We're children of the Living God walking closely with Him and seeking to bring about what He wants, not what benefits us most.

It can be quite annoying when Christians bleat on in December about how the world around them has taken the "Christ" out of Christmas. It's frustrating, as it's another example of the church moaning at the world when we ourselves have not got our own house in order. We need to first make sure that we keep the Christ in Christianity before we start on anyone else. We must not fall into the trap of simply doing sanctified humanism and calling it outreach. Having a load of teenagers in your church playing the PlayStation is not mission in and of itself; neither is a mums and toddlers group that never mentions Jesus. However, these can become good starting points for mission if they are intentional. We need to bring Christ in front and back to all we do as the church.

Growing confidence will allow us not to worry (as we often do) about offending people. After all, if you go into Carphone Warehouse and they try to sell you a phone, you're not offended. Why then would anyone be offended if, when they come into church, we mention Jesus?! We need to be clear about whose we are and make all of our ministry entirely Christ-focused. This does not mean that we're preaching at people all the time but simply that we are not being used as purely a social benefit to people when the greatest thing they need is Christ. Make no mistake: we are not called as the church to build Prime Minister David Cameron's "Big Society" but instead to build Christ's "Big Kingdom". There will be many sociological benefits along the way, but our chief goal must remain the fulfilment of the Great Commission above all else.

It's time we acknowledged that it may be hard but we do need to persevere. Jesus never promised it would be easy; He promised He'd always be with us. The time has come for us to be faithful to Jesus for the rest of our days in the face of a culture that says only do what feels good. We need a reality check that it's not always easy. From Christ on a cross and the early Christians being burnt as candles in Nero's garden or fed to the lions, through to the atrocities of the so-called

Islamic State towards Christians in recent years, we have to face the fact that standing for Jesus is hard and may cost us everything. However He is bigger than any of the opposition, hurdles, or challenges we may face. Others may seemingly win the battle but God has won the war! Therefore we press on and keep going.

For too long the church has been on the back foot, constantly defending the many questions of the world and not really asking any. If a cricketer plays the whole time on the back foot when batting, then the best score possible is 0 not out. However, on the front foot the possibility of scoring runs is unlimited. In order to be game changers we need a church on the front foot instead of the back; one that's not constantly defensive but instead able to make an impact, asking questions of society and living in a way that can't be missed.

A church on the front foot also has the chance to be defined by what it's for, not constantly what it's against. We're sick of being seen as part of something that's anti everything. We're pro Jesus – the most radical, compassionate, and loving figure in human history. Out of this comes boundaries and rules, but it's the relationship we want to be defined by. Any relationship has rules and boundaries – otherwise it's anarchy – but let's be defined by the things we're for, not against. Let's leave behind this constant reality of people seeing the bride of Christ as being against everything. Jesus did not come to start a religion but to bring life. Indeed, as John 10:10 says, "I have come that they may have life, and have it to the full." Our language needs to change. As the American Christian writer and political activist, Jim Wallis, points out, Dr Martin Luther King Jr didn't say, "I have a complaint." Instead he proclaimed, "I have a dream."[10] We need to start extending our imaginations as to what might be possible. Perhaps we need to stop moaning and instead start dreaming of what might be possible in this land. Let's paint a better picture for people, not keep complaining!

It's time for a gear change in our impact in this land; to take hold of what we're really about and see transformation. The pastor Malcolm Macdonald puts it this way, "In Britain, we spend our lives seeking safety, ease and comfort. Yet, the church I read about in the New Testament ran towards sacrifice, servanthood and risk. What is our goal in life; getting our needs met, or laying our lives down?"[11] It's time we fought against safety, entitlement, and comfort and gave everything. After all, we don't know about you but **we'd far rather join Jesus on the dangerous water than stay without Him in the safety of the boat.**

Let's be game changers taking risks for Jesus and bringing hope to a nation in great need of it, sharing absolute truth and love in a world that's trying not to believe in it. In all things let us aim to see the nation of Britain transformed for Christ.

YES! But how?

This book will be split into five sections, outlined below:

Encounter (Exodus 3:1–18) – How can we make space to encounter God? Let us not underestimate how God may choose to encounter us as we seek to meet with Him. We hope and pray that you will be able to prioritize space and time to meet Him and be transformed in every way. We know and believe that incredible things can happen when we spend time with Jesus. We can only be who we are truly born to be when we begin to see the value of building a relationship with the Lord.

Enlist (Exodus 4:1–20 and 5:1) – We don't just want to be left at the point of encounter. In an experiential culture there is a high value on what we feel. However, our heart cry is that we don't just seek out a "holy moment" but are then inspired and transformed so deeply that we cannot remain where we were – that we are compelled to go out and engage with the world in the name of Jesus. Yes, there will be hurdles along the way (not least ourselves) but let's find a way of overcoming them so that we are bold enough to stand up, speak, and move in power.

Everyone (Exodus 17:8–15) – Christianity was never designed to be a solo pursuit. We are so privileged to be part of a huge body of believers, all around the world, seeking to serve Jesus where they are. Let's not be crippled with self-analysis or comparison, but rather find the co-workers that God has called us to minister alongside. We all have a key part to play so that the glory of Christ can be seen.

Equip (Numbers 13:25 – 14:9) – God's heart is that we hear His voice and know that He has and will give us everything we need to keep on answering the call that He has put on our lives. Society throws so many challenges at us, making it tough to discern the way that Jesus is calling us to go. How do we hear the right voice speaking to us, and how can we be the right voice in the midst of the world in which we find ourselves?

Empower (Deuteronomy 34:1 – Joshua 1:11) – We may not see everything in our own lifetimes. We stand on the shoulders of the giants who have come before us and will then need to depend on future generations to continue the work. How do we pass on our mission to those younger than ourselves and release them in order that they can go further than we ever would? Surely the best is yet to come.

Do you want to be a "game changer"?

Writing this book has challenged us at every turn.

The idea of being willing to encounter God and do whatever He asks of us is to be children of deep surrender.

We are a work in progress and we hope you can join us on a quest to live sold out for Him.

May this book play a part in seeing a bunch of Christian game changers rise up to transform this nation in the name of Jesus.

Ready? Let's get our hands dirty, press forward, and bring a greater sense of kingdom in this land. Maybe you'd like to pray the following…

Lord Jesus,

*Thank you for giving me new life. I gladly give it back to you, for you to use for your glory. Please use this book and whatever else you may choose to help me to be a **game changer** for you.*

Amen.

Part 1

ENCOUNTER

Exodus 3:1–18

1

Moses at the Burning Bush

"No past is dark enough to withstand a transforming encounter with God!"

JARRID WILSON

We love exercise but in truth hate gyms! The human body was created to be active and yet in our world of convenience we have found a way to sanitize and sterilize the very act of movement itself. Instead of exploring the great outdoors many can be seen going round and round on the same piece of artificial equipment surrounded by sweaty companions in luminous sportswear. Ears are filled with music or the TV is watched to distract from the pure banality of what is taking place. On the rare occasions that we find ourselves within this life-sapping environment there is no single piece of equipment less appealing than the treadmill. The joy of running whilst sucking in the fresh air and appreciating the scenery that the Lord painted is entirely lost as the monotony of the treadmill kicks in. Rotating rapidly and noisily, this mechanical monstrosity churns away whilst shortening your running stride in the process. We can think of little that is less appealing than running on a treadmill with no variation, views or fresh air.

In some ways life can sometimes feel like that. We find ourselves often waking up, getting the kids ready, carting them off to school, rushing into work, picking the kids up again, cooking the dinner, getting them off to bed, sitting down and trying not to fall asleep, and then getting up the next day and doing it all again. In your life the pattern may well be different to ours (especially if you don't have the kids!), but the repetitive cycle of day to day activities is something we think we can all relate to. Life was never designed to be like this but sometimes it can feel this way. Sometimes it seems like we live to work and pay the bills. A simple state of survival is seen as success in a life that often feels like every different day rolls into one.

MOSES ENCOUNTERS GOD

In Exodus 3 we find one of the single most incredible encounters between God and mankind in human history, yet it doesn't start out looking like it's going to go that way. Moses is plodding about enduring his mundane everyday business. Nothing out of the ordinary seems likely, life feels dull, and there would be no reason for Moses to have any other expectation than that of completing his day's work in order to rest and get up and do it all again. He is shepherding his father-in-law Jethro's flock when he comes to Horeb, the mountain of God. Writer and Bible teacher Phil Moore puts it this way:

> He has shepherded his father-in-law Jethro's flocks for forty years, which means that he has probably been to Mount Horeb a hundred times before. He assumes this thorny patch of mountainous wasteland is nothing more than the "backside of the desert".[1]

There are no initial signs that anything out of the ordinary is going to take place. Moses is going about his business doing what he always does. Once more he finds himself walking over the familiar terrain, with the same flock in the usual fashion. He is on his own equivalent of a rotating treadmill. Forty years is an awfully long time to have been doing the same thing. Why should this day be any different?

However, everything rapidly changes for Moses when he has an incredible encounter with God. What seems normal and bland is dramatically transformed into a life-defining moment. Quickly the previously known ground which seems so "everyday" becomes holy as the angel of the Lord appears to him in flames of fire from within the bush. One thing that's worth clearing up is that burning bushes were not, and indeed are not, an unfamiliar sight in this part of the world. The climate and conditions mean that regularly bushes can spontaneously catch fire and burn themselves out. However, this burning bush was unlike anything seen before. The incredible thing on this particular occasion is that though the bush was on fire it did not burn up (Exodus 3:2). This makes no sense at all, as under these conditions a bush would burn out and be entirely consumed fairly rapidly. It is the very uniqueness of this reality that first attracts and intrigues Moses. It made no sense to him and was seemingly impossible.

As ever when it comes to the miraculous, various theories have attempted to explain why it is that though the bush is burning it is not consumed. All manner of ideas have been put forward, but in reality there is no real credibility or validity to any of them. As theologian Philip Hyatt writes, in the end "all such naturalistic explanations of this narrative are vain".[2] Trying to explain what happens here to Moses logically is fundamentally futile. The reality of what is taking place is in essence a simple one: **the bush is not burning up because this is God Himself**.

Not only does the bush not get consumed by the flames, but the miracle goes further still as God calls to Moses from within the bush and tells him to take off his sandals for he is standing on holy ground (3:5). God reveals Himself to Moses as the God of Abraham, Isaac, and Jacob, and at this point Moses hides his face from the flames (3:6). This mind-blowing encounter with God transforms Moses' life in its entirety. **Acacia bushes riddle the desert and an ordinary, worn-out one is burning with the glory of God, when an ordinary, worn-out man encounters this and burns with the glory of God too**. There can be little doubt for Moses from this moment onwards that the Lord is with him, that He has great plans for him and that Moses himself simply has to play his part. It is this encounter that sets him up to do extraordinary things and reassures him that God is with him in everything.

Without a powerful encounter with God it would have been near impossible for Moses to fully be himself and to step into all that the Lord had for him. He had to respond to meeting God in the bush whilst simply going about his daily business. While striding on his own version of a treadmill, God met with Moses and suddenly everything was different, his perspective changed, and the course of his life would never be the same again. This encounter with God builds on all that has come before. This is not like the Damascus road for Paul, when a God he did not know encountered him with power in a life-changing moment. Moreover, this encounter for Moses is a confirmation of the Lord's presence and power. Put another way by theologian Alan Cole, "Moses brings no new or unknown God to his people, but a fuller revelation of the One whom they have known."[3]

WHAT ABOUT US?

The challenge that so many Christians have in today's busy world is making space and finding time for encountering

Jesus. Everything feels so incredibly time pressured. As the second line of the poem "The Paradox of our Age", by the 14th Dalai Lama, says simply, we have "more conveniences, but less time". We work longer hours in Britain than ever before, waste many more commuting, and are constantly under strain. Sociological demands stress that women must pursue career and family, and men must be active dads and still climb the career ladder. All of this can be brilliant but it does cost time. This time pressure even kicks in from school age, with the taxing exam league tables placing immense and unnecessary strain on young people, their teachers, and families. Everywhere you look the whole world seems to have got itself into a big rush.

Are we genuinely living in such time poverty that we can't make space for Jesus? American Wellness coach Diane Randall says that "Lack of time is more perception than reality.

The problem is the lack of commitment to your priorities after you've set them. People overwork, set time to watch television and surf the Internet, but **many people don't set time to do the things that they say are important to them.**[4] And herein lies the problem. We don't have less time than previous generations; we just choose to spend it differently. The question is, if the Lord wanted to encounter us as He did Moses, would we even notice? Would we hear His voice over the crowd? Have we got ourselves so busy being busy that we might miss Him?

We simply can't afford to miss out on God. Whether we love the variety in our lives or we feel like life is that monotonous treadmill, we can't get away from the reality that we are all busy. Many talk of a day when things will calm down or this busy season may come to an end, but in truth that day often never comes. For example, Anne's mum often talked about all that she was looking forward to about life once she finally retired: the freedom to do more of what she wanted and be free for other things. Yet, just the other day she said to Gavin over a coffee, "You just don't realize how busy retirement is. I've got more on than I had when I was working." Whether this is entirely true or not, it suggests the quiet days ahead may never actually become a reality. Life is seemingly always busy. Therefore, in the midst of the pressures and the challenges we need to make space for Him in our lives. We all find time for the things we prioritize. We have friends who get up at 5 a.m. in order to go to the gym or others who make all kinds of sacrifices to follow a sports team. When we love something we make room for it.

We remember clearly an advert from our childhood for Rotary Watches. In it the slogan was "because time is the most important thing you can possess". If Jesus is a priority in our lives then we will make time for Him. We will give of our time.

That is why we must make space! Jesus involves His Father in His daily life but He also makes space to be with Him on His own. We must make space and time for God. We cannot allow ourselves to be too busy to spend time with the Almighty.

Ever since beginning in ministry we've always valued spending time with the minister whom we trained under fifteen years ago. On one such occasion Gavin travelled down to see him and settled down for a nice coffee in a trendy café. However, the mood of the moment quickly changed when the mild-mannered man known to us became incredibly assertive. He started tackling Gavin's personal relationship with Jesus head on. The questions began flowing: "How often are you silent before God? Do you ever let Him lead the conversation? When did you last spend time with Jesus without an agenda? How often do you take time out and retreat with the Lord? Is your prayer life a monologue or a conversation?"

Gavin was somewhat taken aback by his stern tone but then the minister crystallized the challenge in the form of a strong analogy: "In your marriage would you get away with spending as little time with your wife as you do in your relationship with Jesus?" Gavin was silent so the minister continued: "This isn't a guilt trip but simply a challenge. Relationships don't survive on tiny snippets of time; they need quality time. It's no different with God. You need to invest more time in your relationship with Jesus."

Hard though it was to hear, he was right. Gavin was not investing enough time in his personal walk with Jesus. We're often so busy in the midst of this fast-paced world that we don't make the time, and when we do it's so often such a small amount. As a result of this conversation the challenge was clear: Gavin needed to intentionally make time and space to be with Jesus; otherwise it wouldn't happen. The quiet time is great, and arrow prayers are brilliant, but like any relationship quality time is needed – enough time for significant encounter.

As a result of that day things have changed massively for Gavin. He has found himself having to take time away from others and be alone with Jesus. In his situation this has involved taking up running long distances. He struggles to be still and not fall asleep, but when on a run of 5 miles or so finds that his body looks after itself; he's able to retreat from normal life and simply hang out with the Lord. For others they find it really helpful to block out a day and simply "kick leaves with Jesus". Without aim or agenda simply spending a day with Jesus is so good for our spiritual health. Others still go on silent retreats or to a retreat centre for a break.

However we do it, we need to make space for significant encounter with God. We also need to be prepared for Him to speak and make His presence known in times when we are doing more mundane things. This is precisely what happened for Moses at the burning bush. If we want to be healthy Christians who make an impact for Christ in this land then we need to be those who create space to encounter God and those who also expect to hear from Him in the normal patterns of life. We can often forget that He is omnipresent (everywhere all the time) and, as such, we can **miss out on opportunities to meet with Him in our daily lives**. Whatever you are facing, in any context, He too is there.

The story of Moses in Exodus 3 makes it abundantly clear that faith is often born out of an encounter with God. We need to make space and time in order to have such an authentic and life-changing/giving experience. Without it we will only go as far as our energy and understanding take us, and that will be nowhere near far enough to impact a nation!

DIFFERENT ENCOUNTERS

The former *Dragons' Den* star Duncan Bannatyne's book *Anyone Can Do It* is a great read. Mr Bannatyne is pretty remarkable – an entrepreneur, author, and philanthropist – doing business in hotels, health clubs, spas, media, property and transport (amongst other things). There is something particularly fascinating in his story: Bannatyne meets with God. Deeply moved from seeing poverty in Romania he finds himself suddenly aware that he is not alone and writes, "It was there that God said hello. It was unmistakable: I knew who had come, and I also knew why. It wasn't a spiritual thing, it was a Christian thing. It was profound, and I stood there stunned, considering the offer and thinking about what it would mean." Bannatyne goes on to say that he wasn't ready to live the full Christian life.[5] He encountered God and yet something inside of him felt unable to surrender his life to Him.

It doesn't matter who we are, what we have done, or how far we think we are from God: He still wants to encounter us. It can happen in so many ways and we cannot limit Him with a list of how, where, and when, though there are common occurrences. Some talk of seeing pictures in their minds, while others have physical feelings – like a "bubbling up" inside. For others it is more about words – standing out from Scripture and imprinting in their minds, or words that come clearly into their thinking through a vision, as happened with the disciple Ananais when the Lord called to him: "Go to the house of Judas on Straight Street and ask for a man from Tarsus named Saul, for he is praying" (Acts 9:11). We can also sense God's presence through talking with others or in nature or solitude. The Lord is ready and waiting to meet with His children; the question is, do we want to meet with Him too?

ARE WE OPEN?

Being open to God presents challenges for all of us. We can blame it on being busy, but there can also be the fear that we will not hear what we want to hear. Many of us go through life with a bucket list of things to fulfil, and yet when we encounter God everything changes. When the Lord gets hold of a life nothing is the same again and all previously held conceptions of value and what we want to do with our lives are up for grabs once more. In the end it becomes a matter of trust. Do we trust God enough to make space to encounter Him and to be transformed into His likeness? Do we trust Him enough that, whatever He has for us and whatever He reveals to us, we will go along with? These are big questions and should not be approached lightly.

We were listening to a friend of ours speaking who's a church minister near where we used to live. He was preaching powerfully, and at one point he said that when it comes to trust he's happy to go with a man who successfully predicted His own death and resurrection. Put this way so succinctly, it sums up the situation. Are we really going to trust ourselves ahead of God? The benefit of spiritual hindsight has so often shown in our own lives that the Lord's perspective is far greater than ours. He's always proved Himself to be bigger than the issues in front of us, greater than the critics having a go, stronger than those seeking to oppress, and far more daring than we would ever be. We need to spend time encountering this God in order for us and those around us to be transformed.

If we are going to see the landscape of a nation changed for Jesus, then this will all be born out of an encounter with God. Our own gifts, might, willpower, and elbow grease will only get us so far. An encounter and ongoing encounters with God will be the fuel for the journey. **Everything needs to be born**

out of an authentic and dynamic relationship with Him that then changes our lives. But this all has to come without terms and conditions. The disciples didn't follow Jesus with a set of criteria before they would do it. Paul never asked what his package was for serving Jesus or what percentage might be contributed towards a pension pot. Mary never agreed to carry baby Jesus as long as she never had to leave her home town and step out of her comfort zone. King David didn't refuse to sing worship until all the numerous requests on his rider were fulfilled.

If we want to be game changers then it must be on His terms and not ours. The Lord invites us to draw near to Him and encounter Him. This could then lead to anything. Just after coming to faith as an eighteen-year-old Gavin prayed a dangerous prayer. He told the Lord that he would do "whatever, wherever and whenever for Him". In the years that have followed Gavin has done many things he's loved, some that he's struggled with, and others still that he would never have chosen. However, as they have been God-led and born out of encounter, he has known the Lord's unwavering presence; he has stepped into things he never thought possible and throughout has known that God will provide.

So it seems clear that the real question is, are we up for a deep encounter with God that could change our life and its course entirely? Are we prepared to get off our agenda and onto His? Are we up for sharing with Him the thing He is most jealous for – our time? As you read this there will be many emotions pouring through your body. That's absolutely fine. God calls us to an extraordinary relationship with Him, but we are still human so will have our apprehensions. Don't worry; you're in good company. Are you feeling scared? So was Moses. Do you feel inadequate? So did he. **It is always far better to join Jesus in the midst of the challenge than**

to stay without Him in the safety of your normal life. Are you up for becoming a game changer? Do you want a life-changing encounter with God? Are you prepared to push in and wait even when you may not feel like you are experiencing anything straight away?

YES! But how?

YOU AND GOD

- Take a moment to think and pray about the main things you do each day, or throughout the week, and put these into the boxes shown below based on how urgent and important they are.[6]

	URGENT	Not urgent
IMPORTANT	**Urgent and important**	**Important but not urgent**
Not important	**Urgent but not important**	**Not urgent and not important**

- Looking at your answers, consider whether your perception of what's important, and the reality in your day to day life, are the same thing.
- Are you treating each item boxed above correctly – is everything in the right section? Moreover, does the way you apportion your time match up with how urgent or important things really are?

- Where would you put your relationship with Jesus? Often we discover that spending quality time with Jesus may fit in the top-right box (important but not urgent) and as such won't happen that often even though it's fundamental. Is that true for you? What other things are in that box and being ignored that should actually be given more attention?

- Does anything need changing? Are you spending too much time on things that seem urgent but are actually not that important?

SOME PRACTICAL WAYS TO ASSIST ENCOUNTER

1. Practise waiting on God in silence over a week. Begin with one minute on the first day and add a minute each day until on Sunday you have seven minutes of silence in God's presence, listening to Him. You could do this in the bathroom with the door locked if you need to hide away from distractions!

2. Mark out a day, or half day, in your diary within the coming month – travel to a place with a grand view where you won't be interrupted and make space to appreciate God's creation. You can do this alone, with friends or as a family. Spend some time considering the things in your life. What are the things you care most about? What do you want in the foreground, and what can you leave further away? Put things in order of priority. Pray about it.

3. For a week, try swapping the time you spend on something like TV, social media or a particular hobby, for something else that might connect you with God. It might be reading the Bible, walking and thinking, staring out of the window, going for a drive, or something else.

4. Book a retreat – it might be twenty-four hours or a week, but get your diary out and set aside some time to search for God, expecting that He wants to encounter you. It might involve booking time off work, asking for help with childcare or investing some money. Make a priority of your relationship with God.

GROUP ACTIVITY

You could try this:

1. Share the story of Moses' encounter at the burning bush in Exodus 3 and ask those listening if they want to have an encounter with Jesus (you may ask them to raise a hand or to comment). Then suggest to those responding that God wants to meet with them. Invite them to open their hands in front of them (if they are comfortable) and pray, asking the Holy Spirit to come and reveal more of Jesus to each one of them individually. At the end of the prayer time, if some were struggling, say that God can meet with us anywhere, and even if they have not experienced Him in that place, perhaps it will happen as they head home or even whilst they sleep. It may not be in the way they expect! Moses had no idea he would be on holy ground that day!

2. Perhaps some of them feel challenged to spend more time with Jesus on a daily basis. Challenge them to share with someone and be accountable to how this new habit could develop in their personal life. If you are in a large group, you may ask them to stand as a way of saying, "I mean business with Jesus", and pray for them to find space to be with Him.

Further reading

O. Chambers, *My Utmost for His Highest* (Grand Rapids: Discovery House Publishers, 2012)
S. R. Covey, *The 7 Habits of Highly Effective People* (London: Simon & Schuster, 2004)
S. Lambert, *A Book of Sparks* (Watford: Instant Apostle, 2012)

2
Faith for the Encounter

"Faith is to believe what you do not see; the reward of this faith is to see what you believe."
SAINT AUGUSTINE

Gavin clearly remembers being sat on an uncomfortable floor surrounded by his fellow nine-year-olds. As ever they were having loads of fun at their church group and enjoying the way the Bible was being brought to life by the slightly over eager leaders. The focus that morning was on healing, and they were told to get in a circle of four or five with a leader. Once sat down, the leader started to ask if anyone had anything physical that they wanted healing for. Immediately James tore his sock off to expose the verruca on his foot. "I've had enough of having to swim with a sock on," he declared. "I want God to heal my verruca." Without a moment's hesitation Gavin began to pray for his friend. His nine-year-old mind was full of faith and didn't even consider for a moment that healing might not happen. He closed his eyes extra tightly to try to add some additional vigour to what he was praying and really gave it some!

When he opened his eyes he was blown away. The verruca had totally gone. Gavin was astounded at the power of God and that He still did miracles today. With hindsight we're amazed that He cares enough to do this. Let's be honest for a moment: there are millions of people suffering horrendously all over the world and yet here was the Lord liberating a nine-year-old from the small matter of a verruca that needed to be socked when swimming. However, experiencing God healing someone at such a young age and with such a fundamentally trivial issue had set Gavin up for life in having the faith to believe God will intervene. Maybe it won't be in healing but we often need to remind our adult self to have the faith to believe that the Lord wants to encounter us today.

It was no different for Moses and the Israelites. They had seen some amazing things: a bush burning that wasn't being consumed (Exodus 3:2); the seas parted so that they could cross over on dry ground (Exodus 14:21); a piece of wood turning bitter water sweet (Exodus 15:25); a hard dry rock dispensing life-giving water (Exodus 17:6). The list of miraculous provision and encounter around the time of Moses seems endless. And yet, in between these incredible moments we see the people doubting, afraid, grumbling, complaining, and forgetting so quickly what God has done. Our humanity is so challenging when we think about encountering the Lord. All kinds of things limit our perspective of what He can do and cause us to quickly forget the ways that we have seen Him move. We so often have such short memories of what He has done and such a long one of that which we feel hasn't happened. What we love about Moses is that he goes on crying out to God; when things get tough, he has faith to look to the Lord and believe that He will come through for them again. We too must remember sometimes to look back and know what He has done. Gavin certainly finds himself remembering that healed verruca when he's faced with praying for healing for far more serious conditions today.

THE BATTLE FOR OUR MINDS

We joined Youth for Christ in 2001, running a gap-year programme for young people wanting to grow in their faith and have a go at different areas of youth ministry. Anne remembers chatting for hours to one of the girls who was struggling with her faith. The conversation was frequently dominated with such comments as, "If God is real, why doesn't He speak to me?" "If He is there and He can show Himself, why doesn't He?" The girl became quite angry and her questioning spirit was beginning to eat her up inside. Anne was responding out of necessity and indeed desperation as she longed for her to grow in her faith, not walk away. It has broken our hearts to see so many people over the years leave the church, and Anne was prepared to fight with all that she had to keep this one. Looking back now at these incessant attempts to convince her of how real God is, it's clear that the only thing that actually needed to shift was her faith. She needed to realize that sometimes as Christians "we live by faith, not by sight" (2 Corinthians 5:7). This quote from Thomas Aquinas powerfully sums up the situation that Anne found herself in: **"To one who has faith, no explanation is necessary. To one without faith, no explanation is possible."**

However, God is so much greater than our limited understanding, and He was at work in this girl's life in so many ways at that time even though she couldn't see it. Anne didn't have a hope of making her believe that, because she was looking at it through lenses that were so different. In a sense she had decided that an encounter with Jesus looked, smelt, and sounded the way that she thought it should, so anything outside of that box in her mind was not attributed to God.

The passage with Thomas, after Christ has risen from the dead, is so helpful in regard to faith. The disciples are clear that they have seen the Lord! And yet Thomas says to them, "Unless

I see the nail marks in his hands and put my finger where the nails were, and put my hand into his side, I will not believe it" (John 20:25). Thomas has decided that seeing and feeling like this is the only way that he will be convinced of the reality of the Risen Jesus. Praise Jesus for His graciousness that He would come and show Thomas what he needed to see. However, Jesus doesn't stop there. He adds such an important message: "Because you have seen me, you have believed; blessed are those who have not seen and yet have believed" (John 20:29).

Sometimes we need to cry out to God like Moses did, asking Him to break through our preconceptions and to go back to the simple message of the cross. Even if we don't feel anything, or see anything or read anything profound, we can still stand on the truth of the gospel. The girl above wrestled for about six months with thoughts like Thomas', but in her head she did not get any proof. When the rubber hit the road and she had to make a decision for or against believing in Jesus, she decided to follow Him, with the simplest, clearest thought in her head: "I would rather live with faith in God than have no hope at all." This echoes the words of Jesus when He says, "If you have faith as small as a mustard seed, you can say to this mountain, 'Move from here to there,' and it will move" (Matthew 17:20).

Elijah sees the first resurrection in Scripture in 1 Kings 17 when he cries out for the son who has died who is then revived. Massive though this moment is, it goes on in the background and occurs away from the masses in the upper room of a house. However, it's the faith gained from this instance that gives Elijah the ability to take on and beat 850 prophets of Baal and Asherah a little later on in 1 Kings 18. **God so often does in the small what later he will do in the big!** We think things have to happen in the big first and it just isn't true. Scripture shows us that it begins with small faithful steps. The same is true for the girl in our story here. Her faith was shattered for a short time, but now she has faith built on a rock; it is not built on feelings that will come and go; it is built on the truth that she decided to keep standing on.

UNUSUAL ENCOUNTER

One of the many things we love about our Lord is that, when He encounters His children, it is not how we predicted it would be or how we imagined it to look, sound or feel! Moses is just happily tending his father-in-law's flock on a normal day, when suddenly he sees flames of fire in a burning bush. The first disciples were carrying out their job, fishing, when Jesus entered the scene and transformed their world; they dropped their nets to follow Him and become fishers of men instead (Matthew 4:20). The apostle Paul is headed to Damascus, intent on putting more Christians in prison, when light flashes from heaven (Acts 9:3). In these moments of encounter, their lives are changed forever. The path that they are on is dramatically transformed, and no matter what happens next, they will never be the same again.

What's fascinating is that we never know when or how this is going to happen for people, but the truth is that if they are looking for Jesus, they will find Him. In our ministry we frequently find that we are following a certain pattern with people of when, where, and how we are going to introduce them to the Lord and then He intervenes and does something beyond what we ever expected or imagined.

One lady came to our church for about eighteen months and gradually she opened her heart and life to the Lord. She became part of the Alpha course that was running, and we have eagerly watched her consider the truth of the gospel and whether she wants to walk with Jesus. One week she came to church and said to Anne, "The strangest thing happened last night. I was sitting in my bedroom, after settling all the children to bed, when I just felt compelled to get down on my knees. I don't know how long I was down there and I haven't got a clue what I was saying – it was a language that I have never heard before – but when I finally got up, I felt like a different person." Anne sat there speechless. In her head she hadn't "prayed the prayer" to give her life to Jesus; she had asked just a week earlier who Adam and Eve were and what happened "on the big boat". Anne had not had a chance to explain why Jesus needed to come and the point of His death and resurrection, and yet here she was detailing a powerful encounter with Christ! Eventually Anne said to her, "How did you feel?" to which she replied, "Peaceful and light." Anne went on to explain that she had been filled with the Holy Spirit and had been talking in tongues. She was so excited and overwhelmed. She has since been going through an incredibly tough time, but what we have witnessed is the power of God protecting her at every turn. When she has needed a staff to part the waters, the Lord has given her sentences in tongues that have immediately calmed her.

The reason we write this is to highlight the constant reality that the Spirit of the Living God never works according to our agenda, at a time that we predict or in a way that we expect that He will. In Exodus 15:25 Moses cries out to God; God shows him a piece of wood, telling him to throw it into the bitter water in order to make it sweet. Why wood? How would wood make water sweet and ok to drink? It is so beyond our human understanding. If we listen carefully to the voice of the Lord (Exodus 15:26) we will not encounter a king who conforms to earthly patterns but one who moves in ways far beyond our understanding. The challenge to us is to be open to the encounter in us and in those we serve, so that we can get on board with what He is doing.

ENCOURAGED BY HIS WORD

When we find ourselves in moments where our faith is weak and fragile, testimonies like the one just written revitalize the hope that is in us. God never planned for us to make a journey of faith alone, but to encourage and build up one another and to "give an answer to everyone who asks you to give the reason for the hope that you have" (1 Peter 3:15). This is the reason why we need the Bible too, because as well as others' stories from the here and now, it provides the historical story of the reality of the Father, Son, and Holy Spirit. Reading it, speaking it, and living it all help to increase our faith for encounter. Phil Moore highlights the power of the word of God:

> The life and death of Jesus, as recorded in the gospels; the resurrection, which even atheist historians cannot explain away; the changed lifestyle of people who have trusted Him ahead of you – all these should give you confidence to trust the Lord with what you cannot see, and spur you on to find that "believing is seeing" when you do.[1]

So often we can feel like a ship out in the sea with no sense of where we are headed. Our faith for a new shoreline may have dwindled away. When we dig deep into the Word of God, we find the way ahead, we read the truth of our life in the lives of the ancients, and we draw encouragement when we see how their doubt was transformed into faith. And when we "feel" like God is far away we can read His truth and find an anchor to hold onto. The Bible provides so much of the foundation for our faith because it is there we read about the resurrected Messiah.

We often need to find a greater respect for Scripture too. It doesn't exist to tell us it constantly agrees with us and to simply affirm our decisions. The Bible is not like one of those nodding dogs people have in the back of their cars that will simply nod along with all that we want. The Bible is full of eternal truth that we need to live by and we can't just change it because we don't like it! The wonderful writer Eugene Peterson puts it this way: "We want to use it (the Bible) for comfort, and if it doesn't work comfortably we reconfigure it so that it will."[2] **We need a higher view of Scripture** than this. We need to see it as the authoritative Word of God that changes our lives. It often feels like the growing biblical illiteracy amongst Christians is the most terrifying thing going on in the UK church. We need to know this book, love this book, and live this book.

Our young children love the *Jesus Storybook Bible* by Sally Lloyd-Jones. There are many great portrayals, and it is well worth a look. One of the greatest things is the way that it ends with John writing, "Come quickly Jesus!", which perhaps is really just another way of saying "to be continued".[3] As a family we love this, because it shows that the Bible is not just a storybook with a beginning and an end, but that the journey of faith is alive now and we are part of a story that is still being written until Jesus returns. The hope and joy that floods our children's faces when we watch this reach into their hearts is felt by us too. In 2 Corinthians 3:2–3 Paul writes, "You yourselves are our letter, written on our hearts, known and read by everybody. You show that you are a letter from Christ, the result of our ministry, written not with ink but with the Spirit of the Living God, not on tablets of stone but on tablets of human hearts." We continue encountering the power of the Living God and our stories of faith go on being written on an estimated 2.4 billion hearts across the world. Sometimes it is just a matter of raising faith by reminding ourselves of the truth that Jesus is alive and that He is coming back again!

WAITING FOR ENCOUNTER

One of the biblical themes we find the most challenging is that of "waiting". As a family we have faith for encounter to happen and have been privileged to witness God do immeasurably more than all we ask or imagine. However, we definitely struggle with waiting for God to do what only He can do! It's hard too as we live in such a culture of instant gratification. Growing up, the most successful shop at the end of the road was the television repair shop. These days, even if your TV is HD if it breaks down you simply throw it away. If the zip breaks on your trousers they go in the bin; yet, twenty years ago, you would have sewn on a new one. We are living in fast-moving times in which everything seems so disposable and instant.

The Bible doesn't offer much comfort in this area of not wanting to wait. We are reminded that "Joseph waited 15 years, Abraham and Sarah waited 25 years, Moses waited 40 years, Hannah waited many, many years. Elizabeth waited at least 60 years. Jesus waited 30 years".[4] Waiting is a huge test of faith. As a wider family we have prayed and prayed and waited for God to bring children, marriage partners, healing, salvation, house moves, and so much more. However, reading the number of years of waiting in the Bible, we find ourselves silently begging, "Please not that long, Lord."

One of the biggest challenges in the waiting is holding onto faith and really trusting God to move in power. Bitterness and cynicism can grow up like thorns in a barren land, seeking to strangle us of faith. Doubt and despair can weave themselves together to form a hedge, completely obscuring our view of eternity. Shoots of negative self-analysis can creep up inside, sucking hope out of our being. Holding onto God and seeking His face in times of waiting is so challenging. Combatting these attacks by standing on the promises of the Lord and worshipping Him anyway is a discipline that few find.

We have seen so many lose their faith because they haven't seen God move in a situation and they have ended up believing that He obviously doesn't care about them. Can you imagine the Israelites in Egypt? They must have cried out to God to rescue them again and again and again. We wonder what this did to their faith. Their only hope could be in God – someone far greater than their situation. Then they witness Him come through for them in a way that was far beyond their wildest dreams or imagination: setting them free from Egypt, crossing the Red Sea, being fed daily from heaven, drinking water from rocks, and so on! When the Lord encounters His children it changes their whole world.

FEELING INADEQUATE

A while back Anne stood up at her ordination service and testified to the journey that God has led her on so far. Within it she was able to share how somewhere deep within her was the belief that God only really wanted to use men to lead and that, as she was married, she was in this life to release and support her husband to fly into all that the Lord had in store for him. Somewhere in her subconscious she had buried the fact that the Lord had called her to Bible College, putting it down to the fact that she went there to meet a partner. In reality she has slowly come to see that He has called her too and that she just needed to have faith to believe that He had and was!

Sometimes we can doubt ourselves so much that we completely miss what God wants to do in us and through us. A couple of years ago Anne found herself sitting on her bed on holiday in North Wales and reading Acts 2:18: "Even on my servants, both men and women, I will pour out my Spirit in those days, and they will prophesy." As she read the words she felt a wave rush through her body and the words "and women" hit her so hard. She felt God clearly saying, "Yes, you." She had all kinds of questions for Him – just as Moses did at the burning bush – related to inadequacy and theological understanding, but knew that Jesus was calling her to trust Him anyway. There was, for a long time, a thought buried deep inside Anne that said, "ordination one day", and yet all the beliefs around her had blocked her view.

One of the problems is that we look at people like Moses through rose-tinted spectacles. We see the liberating hero and can easily make such a character inaccessible to us. In unrealistically venerating him we forget the humanity that lay behind the person brave enough to allow God to use him in spite of who he is! The theologian Alec Motyer puts it this way: "If Moses lives in our memories as the towering leader of Israel in deliverance and pilgrimage, **it is well to remember where he started – insecure, uncertain, unprepared, unworthy and un-almost-everything-else!**"[5] **In truth, if God can use Moses then he can use you and me too.** It won't be the same and we won't do similar things, but He can meet you and me where we are at and as the people He has made us.

When we read about Paul in Acts after his encounter with Jesus, he is filled with the Spirit and "Immediately, something like scales fell from Saul's eyes, and he could see again" (Acts 9:18). Yes, he was blinded, and then he could see, but the truth is Jesus wanted him to see in a whole new way. Paul's entire ministry was turned around and he began to minister in a way that he had never dreamt of or imagined. John Newton, the English slave ship master turned Evangelical Anglican minister, wrote such incredible lyrics around this metaphor in the famous hymn "Amazing Grace": "I once was lost but now am found, was blind but now I see."[6]

When we encounter Christ and His power, our faith lenses shift dramatically. All the "stuff" – the insecurity, the doubt, the fear, and the comparisons – begin to melt away and we see more clearly. Don't get us wrong, we are still human and so there are always things that rise up and try to obscure our view again, but the realization that it is "Christ in us, the hope of Glory" becomes an anchor for the soul.

YES! But how?

YOU AND GOD

- Have you ever encountered God at all?
  If not, why not take a look at www.christianity.org.uk and start to enquire further.

- Are you waiting for God? Why not turn your waiting into resting and listen to the track "Come Away" by the band Jesus Culture, from their album *Come Away* (you may be able to access the track online).

- Have you longed for something to change?
  Read Acts 22:16: "And now what are you waiting for? Get up, be baptized and wash your sins away, calling on His name."
  Perhaps there is some "active" encountering that Jesus has for you to do to change your situation.

GROUP ACTIVITY

1. During a time of reflection, you could ask the group how many of them have hidden dreams? Are there things that they have longed to see God do in their own lives but don't believe will ever happen? Why not write those things down and lay them in the middle or at the front of the room face down, as a way of saying, "God I give this to you, I surrender it to you, trusting you with these things in my heart." Or, if they are amongst friends, perhaps they would choose to share what they long for with one other person and pray for each other that they would come into being.

2. In Acts 9:18, "something like scales fell from Paul's eyes" – he could see in a whole new way. He left one way of living

and began a new one with Jesus. In Exodus 3:12 God says to Moses, "I will be with you." When we encounter God, He changes us and touches us in all our mess and transforms us so that we can make a difference for Him. Ask the Holy Spirit to come and meet with the group and begin to whisper truth to them about who they are in Christ, to give them the strength to leave their old life behind, and to "be transformed by the renewing of [their] mind", so that they can know God's "good, pleasing and perfect will" (Romans 12:1–2).

The Father's love letter is a phenomenal tool based on Scripture for sharing God's heart with His children. It is a compilation of Bible verses from the Old and New Testaments, and you can access it at www.fathersloveletter.com

Further reading

A. Guinness, *Immeasurably Deeper* (Oxford: Monarch Books, 2014)

P. Yancey, *Disappointment with God* (Grand Rapids: Zondervan, 2009)

P. Yancey, *The Jesus I Never Knew* (Grand Rapids: Zondervan, 2002)

3
Making Space for the Encounter

"I'm making space for the unknown future to fill up my life with yet-to-come surprises."

ELIZABETH GILBERT

Much of the last decade in our house has been spent changing nappies and grabbing what little precious sleep was available when our little people chose to sleep themselves. The early years of having children can be a real physical challenge and one in which it's frankly enough to simply get up and do it all again the next day. Yes, people have been having children for a long time, but nonetheless it seems like a time when all your freedoms, rights, and space have been stolen in a flash. Therefore, having recently come through this sleep-deprived era, we find this chapter an interesting one to write. If we are brutally honest, when we were deep in sleep deprivation, surrounded by nappies and screams, we would have laughed at the idea of "space" for anything! We say this because we know there are others who are entrenched in the early years and may feel the same way that we did when they read this heading, "Making space for the encounter". The idea of making space to hear

God is so challenging when we struggle even for head space to follow the deep narrative of an entire episode of *Peppa Pig*!

We are conscious that, since our youngest started school, we have rediscovered the faint foreign notion of "quiet time" and have also found that buried underneath the life of little ones is still a hunger and desire for more of Jesus. However, with that precursor in mind, we want to suggest that there is another way to encounter Christ as a young parent, busy worker, overstretched retiree, or anything else.

Recently, Anne asked the mums group at church to chat with the woman next to them about what they were thankful for, and as she invited feedback she found that top of the list was "caffeine"! It made everyone chuckle in agreement. It is fair to say that "baby brain" needs a good wake-up call found in a hot cup of tea or coffee. If you find yourself in a busy season of life we would encourage you: do not be condemned in your walk with Jesus because you are not having a daily "quiet time"; rather, talk to Him whenever and wherever you can. So many of us hang out with God at the kitchen sink, when we drape the washing on the line, are out walking, on the football pitch, in the quick space between meetings, or even on the loo! **We try to grab moments whenever we possibly can to chat to Jesus**. One of the best times is in the car out on the open road – talking, listening, and watching to see and hear what God is doing. Ask Him to keep you alive in Him and to birth a hunger and dependency on Him through the challenges. Rather than feeling guilty for not "spending time" with Jesus, turn it into arrow prayers, telling Him how you feel and what you long for. He hears it all. He wants to be part of all of our lives too, not just restricted to once a day.

Just like with Moses at the burning bush there are moments when God wants to show us something about Himself, and He is not limited by what we are doing or where we are. We don't have to be at a conference or in a church service for the Spirit to reveal something to us. Moses was on the far side of the desert, John was in prison (Revelation 1), Elizabeth was at home (Luke 1), and Daniel was in the lions' den (Daniel 6). Paul gets up in the meeting of the Areopagus and proclaims the truth about the Lord: "The God who made the world and everything in it is the Lord of heaven and earth and does not live in temples built by human hands" (Acts 17:24). Then, a few verses further on he says, "For in Him we live and move and have our being" (17:28). We can be anywhere to encounter God and in any situation. He lives in us and moves through us no matter where we are.

FINDING TIME

We know Jesus was a busy man who, when He was walking the earth, would have an insanely full Outlook calendar, but we cannot ignore the reality that He still prioritized time to retreat to spend time with His Father (Luke 5:16). Making space to encounter God is one of the biggest challenges we face in our Western culture and mindset. The world seems to get busier and faster, with the idea of stopping and resting or being and retreating a luxury that we cannot afford ourselves. We recall from our childhoods playing for hours with friends in the garden, imagining houses out of trees and bushes, meals out of mud and flowers, scoring World Cup Final winning goals in the garden, making shops out of branches, seeds, and boxes. But now we send our children out into the garden and within minutes they are "bored" because there is apparently nothing to do! We can feel frustration at the lack of imagination and the need to see something like a swing or trampoline to be entertained. Even then, it doesn't keep them busy for long! In an increasingly entertainment-driven culture, we must not lose the ability to stop, to imagine, to dream, and to see beyond what others see. The busyness clouds our thinking, takes away our peace, and causes us to lose sight of where we are going.

Our attention spans have been massively impacted by the world we are part of. The ability to focus on a specific task is vital in life, and yet attention spans have been decreasing over the past decade with the massive increase in external communication. In the year 2000 the average attention span was 12 seconds. In 2015 this had gone down to 8.25 seconds, which is less than that of a goldfish, which has an attention span of 9 seconds.[1] This all then has an impact on our ability to focus fully on time with God. Moreover, it's very discouraging to the preachers amongst us that we will have the attention of some of those listening for only 8.25 seconds!

Moses could not have rescued the people out of Egypt and led them towards the Promised Land, without encountering the Lord – not just once, but many times. We cannot rely on one point of clarity with God and then forge our way ahead, thinking we understand it all, getting consumed with the work of the Lord, and missing out on the Word of the Lord. It is interesting that Moses has to reach for God – the mission that he has to do is so challenging that he knows that he cannot do it alone (Exodus 5:22 – 6:13; 6:28 – 7:5 and so it goes on!). God knows that if we are truly living as those who "live and move and have their being" in Him, then the mission that He will lead us into is not one that we can fulfil in our own strength. The cry of the Lord is that we will keep on reaching for Him and He will keep on showing us where to stand and what to do. We can't afford to live out of poverty of relationship with Jesus. We need to press in and prioritize Him.

Our old pastor used to take one day a week to just be with the Lord. Some would argue that he needed to be spending that time with his flock; however, as a result of his retreating with Him, we knew as a church what the Lord was saying to us and where He was leading us. When the pastor would preach, we knew that He had heard God, because He had made space for encounter. There are different seasons in our life – some where the mere notion of a retreat day is impossible – but when we are able to set aside time for Jesus, the challenge is not to find excuses. We have discovered that there are always times when we are alone – it is how we choose to spend that "alone" time. Even if it's just the walk home from the school gate or the journey into work, we all have time to meet with God. The lure of social media, Costa Coffee with a friend, TV, tablet, apps and jobs is huge, but they must not take us away from worshipping the Lord. What you prioritize you always find time for.

As you read this we pray that your hunger for time with God will be stronger than your hunger for these other things. If it isn't, begin to **ask God to birth a new hunger in you** for more of Him and begin to sacrifice a chunk of time to chat with Him. When the Pharisees are trying to catch Jesus out with questioning His knowledge of the Law, He is very clear in His response as to what really matters: "Love the Lord your God with all your heart and with all your soul and with all your mind" (Matthew 22:37). We can overcomplicate Christianity at times but in many ways it's profoundly simple – **love God, spend time with Him, and pursue His ways**. Pursue Jesus and don't be drawn away from Him by the plethora of distractions around. The enemy is subtle in his distraction but he knows how to tempt you to worship the web or the TV. He knows you have a dilemma with your time and will do whatever he can to convince you to choose a god of this world rather than Christ. If the Lord is God, make space for Him, and try to love Him with all you've got.

CREATING HEAD SPACE

This space is not just about making time in our diaries, but making space in our minds too. We can have all the time in the world, but mentally we are just consumed. One of our friends finds that when he settles down to relax at the end of the day he cannot, because his mind spins with all that has happened in recent hours and all that he has to do for the next day. Coupled with that is a confused batch of emotions in relation to family challenges, which sometimes overwhelm him. If the emotion isn't overwhelming, he may still find that the anxiety linked to these family issues stops him from sitting still or being alone. The idea of making space to encounter God is, in his head, impossible and sometimes even scary.

Some of us can relate to the busyness of mind, others to the anxiety, but Jesus still desires to meet with us, not because He wants to control His children but because He loves us so much. The devotional book *Jesus Calling* has blessed Anne so much, and a recent entry read, "A mind preoccupied with planning pays homage to the idol of control."[2] When our minds are full of stuff, we cannot hear the voice of God. The busyness begins to dictate our whole life, even the moments of quiet! What is amazing is that we don't have to fight our way through a mind full of thoughts in order to encounter God, because the gift of the Holy Spirit can help us to tune our minds to God and tune out the excessive thoughts and planning.

All of us find different ways to unwind mentally, but one of the keys is offloading your thoughts, feelings, and plans at the foot of the cross – a metaphorical transfer of "mental stuff" from you to the feet of Jesus. This may need to be an out-loud rant, especially if you are someone who works out your thoughts externally; for others it may just be naming individual concerns and imagining yourself handing them to Jesus. Coupled with this is a prayer: "Holy Spirit, lift these plans and concerns from my mind, so that I can encounter you."

When both of us spend time with the Lord we take a little while offloading "stuff" and then the rest of the time listening to what the Lord might want to say. When Anne met with a friend recently she gave her space to offload what was on her mind, and then Anne had the privilege of witnessing her have a terrific Holy Spirit encounter. She was overwhelmed, not with anxiety but with peace that truly did transcend our understanding. **When we make space for encounter, the Lord breaks through and changes everything** – our perspective, our feelings, our view of ourselves – and moves us to a place of believing for more.

ENCOUNTER ON-THE-GO

Space for encounter is not just about us talking to God, but listening and receiving from Him too. The more we pray like this, the more we respond to what He is doing wherever we are. Jesus is no longer just someone that we hang out with in the quiet place, but we see more and more that we are taking Him out into the world and into every situation in which we find ourselves. The encounter that Moses has at the burning bush does not end there; it begins something new. When they take Aaron's staff before Pharaoh, it turns into a snake and eats the sorcerers' staffs (Exodus 7:8–12). Moses carries the truth from the place of encounter into reality; he doesn't just see the power of God in the burning bush but played out in front of him in the world.

We can so often talk to Jesus when we are alone but forget that we have access to Him and His power working through us all the time. Our pastor, Shaun Lambert, reminds us of how the Son of God ministered:

> When he heals the paralytic some teachers of the law are thinking judgementally of Jesus, and we are told, "Immediately Jesus knew in his spirit that this was what they were thinking in their hearts" (Mark 2:8). This insider view is traditionally ascribed to a gift of discerning through the Holy Spirit. It is also a product of His spending time in prayer – the crucible of becoming aware.[3]

Here we see that the interaction between the Father, Son, and Holy Spirit was so immediate and consistent. Jesus retreated to spend time with the Father and yet here He is ministering and yet still fully engaged in encounter with the rest of the Godhead. When we make space to encounter God, we get to know Him better, we begin to see Him more, and we hunger to engage in His work wherever we are.

Anne was meeting someone at church and they were sharing their heart. She knew that in a short time they would find space to pray. However, instead of waiting for the "prayer moment" she just began to shoot up some arrow prayers in her mind: "Lord, will you increase the presence of your Holy Spirit in this conversation"; "Lord, please show me what is important here"; "Lord what do you want to do?" The tone changed in her from being one of "What is troubling her and how can I help?" to "I need counsel from above now." As they talked words and thoughts came out of Anne that clearly came from Him. She was privileged to hear and see things that she wasn't saying. The Lord ministered powerfully through her that day, and the other woman's thinking was transformed by the Holy Spirit. This is relevant in any context too. A friend of ours is a police officer and he's spoken before about praying whilst interviewing suspects in order that the Lord might help him. **Wherever, whatever, and whenever, the Lord is with us and ready to listen to our prayers**.

Without conversation with the Lord, we rely so heavily on ourselves and our own abilities. But when we turn to Him, we are aware of so much more and we can witness Him "move mountains" in people's lives. Making space to encounter God can happen in the quiet place but it can also happen in the midst of conversation; we just have to choose to look to Him. After considering God's power in Exodus 17:8–13 and noting how He "supernaturally intervenes" on the battlefield with Joshua and Moses, the American pastor Bill Hybels helpfully writes this:

Moses discovered that day that God's prevailing power is released through prayer. When I began praying in earnest, I discovered the same thing. It boils down to this: if you are willing to invite God to involve Himself in your daily challenges, you will experience His prevailing power – in your home, in your relationships, in the marketplace, in school, in the church, wherever it is most needed.[4]

DIGGING DEEPER

The theologian Krish Kandiah refers to being at the supermarket at a time of day when he is hungry and thus stocking up on unhealthy treats, knowing that the healthy ones are important but passing them by. He says that our approach to the Bible can be similar: "We often come to the Bible spiritually peckish, and satisfy ourselves temporarily on some unhealthy takeaway moral. But what we need is the raw materials for the healthy long-term diet God wants to feed us with, packed with invisible vitamins and minerals that will make us spiritually strong."[5]

To encounter the fullness of the Godhead, we need to feast on the whole picture – Old Testament and New. It is not a question of reading our favourite bits only but finding the patience to soak in the story, asking the Holy Spirit to illumine the text so that it lives before our eyes. We may need to start taking the Bible more seriously and seeing it for what it truly is. The pre-eminent leader of the Indian independence movement in British-ruled India, Mahatma Gandhi, said, **"You Christians look after a document containing enough dynamite to blow all civilisation to pieces, turn the world upside down and bring peace to a battle-torn planet. But you treat it as though it is nothing more than a piece of literature."**

We need to develop a real taste for the Word of God, to feast on it and go deeper with it. There are many ways to do this but one you may find helpful to try is *Lectio Divina*, a dynamic way of reading the Holy Scriptures that has been around since AD 300. It encompasses a four-step approach of reading, meditation, prayer, and contemplation.[6] If you push through with it you will hear from the Lord and it will work for you (there's more on this in the "Yes! But how?" at the end of this chapter).

All of this is so countercultural. There is a constant battle with a culture that says, "Satisfy yourself with whatever you want. Try it once but then chuck it away after that if you feel bored." God wants to keep showing us new things in His Word; He wants to keep revealing fresh stuff that the Spirit is doing. The challenge is not to quit anything quickly. Our God is in the business of a loving relationship; He is not a one-hit wonder who will then disappear. We have often read the same passage over and over again but then there will suddenly be a moment where it reads differently and a word or phrase will stick out in a way that it has never done before!

If you can make space to encounter God in your daily life, it will change you and everything that you touch and do. Moses is just one testimony of a changed life. If we take a risk and prioritize Jesus, life will never look the same again. Bill Hybels gives us a poignant reminder of life without prayer:

> *Prayerless people cut themselves off from God's prevailing power, and the frequent result is the familiar feeling of being overwhelmed, overrun, beaten down, pushed around, defeated. Surprising numbers of people are willing to settle for lives like that. Don't be one of them. Nobody has to live like*

that. Prayer is the key to unlocking God's prevailing power in your life.[7]

Our prayer is for a hunger in your heart for God that is far greater than your desire for everything else.

YES! But how?

If all of this is confusing you and you don't even know where to begin, check out www.trypraying.org. Here you will find some very simple ways and lots of help to start talking to God.

However, if you are further on than this…

YOU AND GOD

Ask yourself: have you got stuck in a certain "formula" for spending time with God? Perhaps it is time to try something different?

Try a new way of reading the Bible…

Have you heard of *Lectio Divina*?[8]

Lectio is the way we read the text; it goes deeper than we will ever fathom!
Mediato is when we meditate on it – we enter into the world of the text.
Oratio is praying "let it be done according to Your Word".
Contemplato is naturally living out the Word of God.

For example: John 20:11–18, "Jesus appears to Mary Magdalene":

- Pray over the text, asking the Holy Spirit to illumine the words (see Revelation 2:7: "Give me ears to hear what your Spirit is saying to me, as part of your church").

- Read it; imagine what it looks, sounds, and smells like. What jumps out at you?

- Perhaps meditate on Mary with her long hair over her face, soaked with tears, her back turned on the "gardener", struggling to see through swollen eyes. Oh, maybe that is why she doesn't immediately recognize him! But then He says her name – **in Aramaic** (verse 16) – in her tongue, in a language she understands, and in a way that she knows it is Jesus!

- What is God saying to you through the words? There will be multiple layers. Perhaps just one or two words, or a phrase, may speak to you. When Jesus calls our name, whatever state we are in, we know that it is Him. Then we see the first evangelist run to tell the disciples, "I have seen the Lord!" What is God calling you to do with what He has shown you today?

- Then pray, "Lord, let it be done in and through my life."

Try a new way of praying...

Have you ever delved deeper into the Lord's Prayer? In his book *Building a Discipling Culture*,[9] Mike Breen opens our understanding of six areas for prayer within Matthew 6:9–13.

A way to pray it through:

1. The Father's character (verse 9): **Our Father who is in heaven, hallowed be Your name**
   "God, we worship you as Abba Father – thank you that you transcend physical separation and enable us to have a relationship with you. You are holy. You are other. We want to be like you…"

2. The Father's kingdom (verse 10): **Your kingdom come, Your will be done on earth as it is in heaven**
   "Lord, we long that your kingdom would come where we are, throughout this nation, and in this whole world. Our hearts cry out for your will to be done – that the truth of the cross would lead people into forgiveness as they encounter your love and are transformed."

3. The Father's provision (verse 11): **Give us today our daily bread**

   "Oh Lord, thank you for providing for us. We remember all those who need daily bread today… please meet all their needs. Father, we need strength mentally, emotionally, physically, and spiritually – will you come in power and equip us to shine for you."

4. The Father's forgiveness (verse 12): **Forgive us our debts, as we also have forgiven our debtors**

   "Father, forgive us. Show us where we are sinning and cleanse us in our thoughts, words, and deeds. Father, who do we need to forgive? Please help us to forgive others and not to keep holding grudges."

5. The Father's guidance (verse 13a): **Lead us not into temptation**

   "Lord, please help us to live differently – to avoid temptation and to take the message of the cross out into the world in power and with authority."

6. The Father's protection (verse 13b): **And deliver us from the evil one**

   "Lord Jesus, we know that the evil one comes to steal and kill. Please will you protect us by the power of your name and help us to stay focused on the mission that you have called us to, Amen."

The great thing with this way of praying is that you can use the verses as triggers and then elaborate in conversation with God in the way that you feel led to. You may have a specific person in mind as you pray – "Lord, please let your kingdom come in Jack's life, deliver him from evil, for your glory", or as you pray you may only get through the first part of the Lord's Prayer because you just want to worship Him and lift up His name. Jesus gave us such a rich way of praying with these verses.[10]

GROUP ACTIVITY

1. Could you create space to encounter God? Turn off phones, get as comfy and silent as possible! Take a few minutes to encourage people to share their questions/concerns/fears with Jesus. Maybe this is an "out loud" moment, like Moses to God: "What if they do not believe me or listen to me and say, 'The Lord did not appear to you?'" (Exodus 4:1), or "I have never been eloquent, neither in the past nor since you have spoken to your servant" (4:10) and "Pardon your servant, Lord. Please send someone else" (4:13). Then, when this is off their chest, allow some quiet and ask the Holy Spirit to reveal truth to the group; let them listen to the Lord's reply.

2. Why not use the Lord's Prayer above, by way of response? You could say the lines and give space after each one to interact corporately.

   For example, say, **Our Father who is in heaven, hallowed be Your name**, then encourage everyone together to say their praise and thanks out loud to the King.

   Say, **Your kingdom come, Your will be done on earth as it is in heaven**, then ask them to call out the places and people where they long to see God intervene.

   Say, **Give us today our daily bread**, then corporately and quietly thank God for His provision, followed by offering to Him the areas and people that you know need His daily bread today.

   Say, **Forgive us our debts, as we also have forgiven our debtors**, then, if everyone is comfortable getting on their knees or sitting down, give them a moment to ask God to show them where they need His forgiveness and ask Him to help us to forgive one another. There may be an outworking of this after the group time – encourage them to see it through afterwards.

Say, **Lead us not into temptation**, and pray protection over the group while they are sat – asking God to protect their minds, hearts, bodies, etc. and to seek lives of holiness and purity.

Finally say, **And deliver us from the evil one**, and pray for the full armour of God over their lives, from Ephesians 6:10–18.

Ask all this in the name of the Lord God Almighty, Amen.

Tip: You could use *The Message* version of the Lord's Prayer and adapt the interactive bits. Communion would be a great visual aid as you walk through the daily bread and ask for forgiveness.

Further reading

G. Fee, D. Stuart, *How to Read the Bible for all it's Worth* (Grand Rapids: Zondervan, 2014)

K. Kandiah, *Route 66* (Oxford: Monarch Books, 2011)

S. Young, *Jesus Calling* (devotional) (Nashville: Thomas Nelson Inc., 2007)

Part 2

ENLIST

Exodus 4:1–20 and 5:1

4
Are You In?

> "A person who doubts himself is like a man who would enlist in the ranks of his enemies and bear arms against himself. He makes his failure certain by himself being the first person convinced of it."
>
> AMBROSE BIERCE

A few years ago we remember saying to one another that we would love to write a book about everything that had just happened to us. It was after the journey of pregnancy and childbirth – a roller coaster never to be forgotten. Losing a baby, nearly losing another one, blood transfusions in utero, premature birth – the list of challenges was a long one. We felt a strong desire to share the story, not to make the world aware of our difficulties, but to proclaim how incredible Jesus had been to us at every turn. Every now and then we would have the thought of writing a book at the back of our minds. Sometimes we would let it fester for a little bit and entertain a title or perhaps who we would like to endorse it, but after a while the thoughts would get buried. There were all kinds of reasons why we would keep on ignoring the idea – nearly always because we were "too busy". We remember pushing the dreams down deeper, with thoughts like "Who do we think we are to write a book about us?", "No one will read it", "What difference would it make?", and "We are better off just praising God for what He has done through all of this."

So many of us have ideas or thoughts like this – some that we might have once and then never again, and others that keep reoccurring in our minds – and yet for all kinds of reasons we allow our thought process to bury them as deep as we can. We find ourselves dreaming of what could be, or thinking "if only things were different, we might…" We bury some of these ideas because we just do not believe that we could ever see them through. We doubt ourselves. We doubt God and we question whether our circumstances would even allow us to carry out our dreams. There are occasions where we may entertain our ideas for a little bit longer – perhaps we talk about them with a friend or a partner, maybe we journal about them on holiday – but at the end of the day we lay them to rest; it is just not possible with the life that we have.

You could argue that our doubts and distractions are a real obstacle to our encounters with God being able to properly ignite. Perhaps we are headed towards the burning bush, open and ready to hear from God, but **the minute the flames become real, we throw cold water on them and walk away**. Some of us do this for years. Others cannot lay our thoughts to rest so we have to wait and listen. Others still doubt so deeply that we don't even allow the bush to begin to burn – the spark inside us keeps being stamped out.

What we love about Moses is that he is like us. His encounter at the burning bush begins with an open heart and mind: "I will go over and see this strange sight – why the bush does not burn up" (Exodus 3:3). He is curious to see what is happening before his eyes; he is attracted to the supernatural, and hungry to meet with God. And yet the eagerness quickly turns into fear when in chapter 4 we discover a man that is ready to bury the encounter as deep as he can. He doubts how people will receive him, he questions himself, and he wishes God would choose someone else. Our humanness is fascinated with the supernatural and powerful nature of God, but the question is, how many of us are prepared for the cost? It is one thing to want to see and know God at work in our lives, but will we sacrifice our own agenda to see more of His kingdom come? The people whom we admire, who minister with the power and authority of God, are the ones who have accepted the cost, who have been willing to face their fears and to step out in the valley.

Let's look at Moses' encounter a bit closer: the Lord God Almighty shares an incredible plan with Moses – a plan to set his people free, to rescue them from the Egyptians, to be with him no matter what – and He reassures His son that He has seen all that has happened to the Israelites. It's amazing that God would choose Moses to work through to bring this about! However, Moses is no longer a trusting, open soul; he is suddenly afraid.

HIS EXPERIENCE

We hear his first reaction in Exodus 3:11: "Who am I that I should go to Pharaoh and bring the Israelites out of Egypt?" To put it in another way, Moses' position was, "Look, I am not up to the job. You shouldn't have picked me." The Lord's reply was, "Of course you are not up to the job. I knew that when I chose you for it. **The point is not your ability but mine!**"[1] Moses thinks so little of himself in this situation and cannot believe that God would choose him, and yet he is the perfect man for the job. His whole life so far points to this moment. He himself has been rescued from death – born a Hebrew, set out on the water in a waterproof basket, saved by Pharaoh's daughter and raised in an Egyptian household as a son of Pharaoh (Exodus 2:1–10). Just as Moses was rescued, God wants to use Moses to rescue more lives. His understanding of Egyptian life is no accident; in fact, it serves him well to go to Pharaoh – a life and a family that he knows and has journeyed with. Moses bridges the gap between the Israelites and the Egyptians. Even though he cannot see it, God sees that now is the time for Moses to do what he is called to do. The experience that Moses has had has equipped him to save God's people.

Hindsight is a beautiful yet frustrating thing, isn't it? It's those "aha" moments, when we realize why we have faced what we have faced, when we can see the hand of God over our lives so far and how He has moulded and shaped us for key roles and tasks at perfect times.

A few years ago Anne was sitting with our pastor in our lounge chatting over a cup of coffee about life and the future. It was just a relaxed conversation, but bit by bit she could feel a sense of churning happening inside of her. It wasn't the first time she had felt like that; it had been coming on her every now and then when she was really praying and surrendering her life to God afresh. If you don't want to really live for Jesus, don't start offering Him your life! We love that bit in the film *Evan Almighty*, where Evan tells God that he wants to change the world for Him, but little does he realize that, from that moment, God is going to take him at his word and change the whole course of his destiny! As a smart, respected congressman, he begins to build an ark and the rest is history. It is well worth a watch, but challenging in respect to what happens when we choose to truly give our lives to God.

So Anne is sat comfortably in a chair, when the churning begins again and the conversation turns into prayer. Our pastor turns to Anne and, eyeball to eyeball, says: "I believe God is saying that it is time to metaphorically go down to the shed at the bottom of the garden and unlock it and take out your tools. He wants you to take them out of the toolbox, clean them up, get rid of the dust, and begin to use them again." The tears rolled down Anne's cheeks because she knew God was calling her, not to remain comfortable, not to just settle where she was. It was a Moses moment for two reasons. First, she was suddenly aware that her experiences and journey so far had already provided the tools that were needed to begin to do what He was calling her to do. Second, the question "Who am I?", which Moses spoke, pretty much summed up the feelings in Anne's stomach. She could think of every reason possible why it shouldn't be her!

The bottom line is that there is a price tag to following Jesus; it was never meant to be easy. We live in a consumer entitlement society, where "what I can get" is often the focus. If my life ticks the boxes, then God is surely with me. If I am comfortable, safe, and popular, then I am "getting it right" with Jesus. Our experience has shown us something entirely different: following the King of the World requires sacrifice. It means laying down our own agenda bit by bit, piece by piece, and asking God to equip us to walk in His way. This is not about punishment but about intimacy with the Author of Life – as we get closer to Him we see and understand more of who we are and we surrender to Him, dependent on Abba Father to work through us for His glory.

In his book *Strengthen Yourself in the Lord*, American Pastor Bill Johnson scripturally considers David and helpfully says, "God did not bring the man after His own heart straight from the pasture to the palace. **Incredibly, David did not assume the throne until 10–13 years after Samuel had anointed him to be King**. In those interim years, David endured more difficulty, persecution and rejection than many of us face in a lifetime."[2] Just like Moses, who went from shepherding a literal flock of hundreds to an Israelite flock of thousands, it took time, change, and growth. Whatever our journey, we can rest assured that God uses everything we face to make us ready for that moment of encounter, so when we get to the place of "Who am I?" God wants us to see that His hand has already been at work, filling your box with tools. Not everything will be to hand, because if it were, then we would get on and do it, without needing the Lord at all. Jesus still wants us to depend on Him – it is He who brings breakthrough, not us.

OTHER PEOPLE

Moses is such a great example to us of ourselves. A child reading the story could be forgiven for thinking, "What is Moses' problem? He is face to face with a burning bush, hearing God speak audibly and clearly over what He wants him to do, and yet he constantly questions Him! If it were me, and I was seeing and hearing that clearly, I would just get on and do it!" However, a mature reader realizes how hard it must have been for Moses to do what God was asking him to do. The dialogue is more complex than it may first appear, and the human spirit is weak and fragile. Stepping out into the will of God is a process that often involves lots of questioning and can be really tough.

One of the biggest hurdles for Moses is other people. He is worried about going to the Israelites because of how they will respond, what they will say, and whether they will believe him (3:13; 4:1). Our perspective of what other people may think and feel can cripple us to the point of not being able to act at all. Interestingly, it is all pre-empted – Moses is worrying about the Israelites and Pharaoh before he has even left the burning bush.

We have such a decided view of how people will react to us, and we are terrified to step out and do or say what we feel led to. And yet, if we stay where we are – "in the boat", as John Ortberg refers to it – we give in to fear, we limit our growth, we never live the life that we could have lived with God. We will never know what they will say, until we say it to them. Orberg writes, "Those who say no to God are changed too. They become a little harder, a little more resistant to His calling, a little more likely to say no the next time. Whatever the decision, it always changes a life – and it changes the world that little life touches."[3]

Is our fear of what people will say and do greater than our fear of not living life for Jesus? It is so challenging. Thankfully, Moses demonstrates a life that says "yes, I will go", even though he reveals his questions.

When Anne was speaking at a church recently, they were looking at David and Goliath and how astounding it is that all the Israelite soldiers are terrified of this giant Goliath, and yet David faces him head on, knowing that God is on his side. Anne was sharing how our fear can prevent us from facing people that we need to face, and saying or doing what we know we should do. After a moment of reflection and prayer, one of the congregation came to Anne and said, "I know I need to go and speak to someone, but I am afraid." They prayed together. In a matter of only a couple of hours she called Anne to say, "You won't believe it, but circumstances meant that I had to face the individual this afternoon! I had the courage and strength to say what I needed to say, and it was absolutely fine!" The conversation was nothing like the woman had predicted; in fact it went the opposite way – it brought them closer together and liberated her, giving her greater courage for future conversations with others.

God doesn't ask Moses to go to the Israelites and to Pharaoh to upset him, or to cause him to suffer; He does it to help him grow. The reality is that "before Goliath, David fought a lion and a bear. Every battle is designed to train, prepare and build confidence."[4] David and Moses say "yes" to God, and because they do, they are changed. Their dependence and intimacy with God deepen and their character and courage develop.

ABILITY

It is amazing how honest and aware Moses is of his failings and fears. Instead of keeping them inside him and then walking away, Moses gets them all out into the open. He doesn't hold back or run away, but faces himself and God, head on. There is something so powerful and so necessary about being authentic with the Lord – about laying our lives out before Him, turning over the stones of doubt and fear – so that we can truly let Him shine His light and truth into every circumstance. No matter how weak and rubbish we think we are, Jesus is with us, and He does it through us. We do not need to rely on ourselves.

Moses says to the Lord, "I have never been eloquent, neither in the past nor since you have spoken to your servant. I am slow of speech and tongue." The Lord replies, "Who gave human beings their mouths?... Now go; I will help you speak and will teach you what to say" (Exodus 4:10–12).

We have such deep doubts about whether Jesus will come through for us, and yet He is always faithful to His children. Sometimes we wonder if the thing that we think is the weakest in us, is the one thing that God wants to use the most – not to give us a hard time, but to show the world that it is He and His glory working through our lives.

Then we have the final heart cry of Moses: "Please send someone else" (Exodus 4:13). At this point we see the depth of Moses' lack of belief in himself and in what he can do. We are plainly aware that he thinks that someone else would be better than him. We see clearly that, on every level, he does not want to go. Moses is without a doubt a reluctant leader and yet the truth is before us: God has chosen him.

This gives us hope and fear. Those people that we have been looking at for years and thinking that they are so much better than we are, so much more capable; those folk that we have been relying on to do God's work in our place, have a different part to play. **God is calling you to do something and be someone that no one else can be**. He wants to take the "weak things of the world to shame the strong" (1 Corinthians 1:27). He builds His church on people who doubt like Moses, who deny Him like Peter, who have persecuted Him like Saul. Nothing that we have faced is wasted; it can all be turned around and forgiven and used for God's glory.

PROVISION

When we say "yes" to Jesus and engage with the mission that He has put before us; when we stop burying our dreams and running from the Holy Spirit encounter that we know Christ has for us, we can know for certain that He will provide all that we need and He will not let us down.

We love the fact that after all Moses' questioning God says

to him that he can take his brother Aaron with him (Exodus 4:14–16). God sees exactly into our hearts and knows exactly what we need to succeed. We may have to step out and trust before we see it, like Peter on the water (John 14:22–32), but if we fix our eyes on Jesus we will see and do incredible things.

Moses is not suddenly confident after his encounter with the Lord, but he has found reassurance and encouragement in the words "I will be with you" (Exodus 3:12) and "I will help you speak" (Exodus 4:12). God also shows Moses physical miracles with his staff (Exodus 4:2–5) and with his own flesh (Exodus 4:6–8). Finally, God provides help in the form of Moses' brother, Aaron (Exodus 4:15, 27–30). The words, actions, and deeds of the Lord God Almighty equip Moses to step out and begin the work that He is calling him to do.

If God wants you to step out and do something for Him and it is in His timing, you can rest assured that He will have moved everything into position for His plans to come to pass. We love the book of Esther and the way that her "father" Mordecai (2:7) speaks prophetically into her unlikely situation in the palace: "If you remain silent at this time, relief and deliverance for the Jews will arise from another place, but you and your father's family will perish. And **who knows but that you have come to your royal position for such a time as this?**" (4:14). Mordecai can see that the Lord has moved everything into place for Esther to make a real difference for the Jewish people and he is determined that she will not miss it. It is an incredible story of a woman who must have felt afraid like Moses, but who still wisely and courageously stands up for and liberates her people (8:16–17).

The question is, has God moved you into a position for "such a time as this"? Is there something that He has for you to do now? It could be that the enormity of the task looks a little bit like Moses going to Pharaoh or Esther going to King

Xerxes, and the idea of it is overwhelming. However, if the Lord has ordained it for this time, then you can trust Him completely to come through, just as He did for them. Look around you; there will be people ready to go with you.

The book idea that we had buried deep inside us did eventually get written. We got over ourselves and realized that God wanted to use our story to minister to others, and the publisher was interested to pursue it. There was a "right time" for us to see *Stumbling Blocks* come into print and, thanks to Jesus, it was a dream that became a reality. You just need to look at your hands: what has God put in them for you to use? What is in your heart to do? It may well not be a book. It may be inviting your neighbour to something at church. It might be starting to pray at lunchtime in your workplace. It could be handling your finances and life totally differently. Whatever it is in your context, remember: He is with you and He will help you to do it. Pray, pray, and pray again!

YES! But how?

YOU AND GOD

> ## "YOU ARE NEVER TOO OLD TO SET ANOTHER GOAL OR TO DREAM A NEW DREAM."
> ### – C. S. LEWIS

Make a list of dreams you had for the future when you were a child, or at least younger than you are now. Have you achieved any of them? Consider whether any of them are still dreams worth chasing or if it's time for new ones. Is there something you want to happen in your sphere of influence? Identify the goal, and then try breaking down the steps it would take to make it happen. Decide what the first step is and resolve how to take action on that one.

- Have you buried a dream under a wave of reasons?
- Is it time to see if it can happen?
- What is holding you back?
- Why not pray about it, asking God if He can help you to make it a reality?

Martin Luther King, Jr dreamt of seeing something incredible when he stood up and gave his famous "I have a dream" speech at the Lincoln Memorial in 1963. He had a vision of overcoming huge prejudice and inequality so that his children and future generations would live in a society that did not judge them for their race. He was realistic about the challenges and hurdles to be overcome, but in the face of difficulties still proclaimed and held onto his dream.

If you had to share your dreams – what you long to see in your lifetime or beyond – what would you say? King says, **"Even though we face the difficulties… I still have a dream."**

These dreams are unique and God-given. They are not impossible with Jesus.

GROUP ACTIVITY

1. **What is holding you back?** Share Exodus chapter 4 with the group. Highlight the different challenges and questions that Moses had but then emphasize that it was God that changed history through Moses; he just had to say "yes". Ask the group to consider what holds them back. Give them some paper and/or some space to think about it. Perhaps suggest, "Is it not feeling good enough? Is it about what others may think of you? Is it what could happen if you went ahead?" Write down the things that hold them back. Then pray over the group, asking God to lift these burdens off them. Encourage them to rip up the paper and scatter it in front of them. Ask them to stand and then pray for confidence and courage over the group. Remind them that as God gave Moses His mouth, He gave us all we need.
Play or sing "You make me brave", by Amanda Cook and Bethel Music. (You may be able to access this online.)

2. **What is in your hand?** God gave Moses a staff; He also gave him Aaron and others to help him on his mission. Remember the tool shed from this chapter? God has given us what we need. Ask Jesus to show the group what He has put in their hands. Give some space for each individual to hear from God. You could begin to tell them what you think God has put into their hands. Then you might encourage the rest of the group to begin to share with one another what they see that Jesus has given them; for example, the ability to listen, to care, to speak up, to write, to paint, etc. Pray that they will begin to have courage to use what is in their hands and discover new gifts that Jesus has anointed them with.

Further reading

D. Bonhoeffer, *The Cost of Discipleship* (London: SCM Press Ltd., 1959)
Watchman Nee, *What Shall This Man Do?* (CLC Ministries, revised edition 1998)
R. Warren, *The Purpose Driven Life: What on earth am I here for?* (Devotional) (Zondervan, 1997)

5
Overcoming Hurdles

"A lot of people give up just before they're about to make it. You know, you never know when the next obstacle is going to be the last one."

CHUCK NORRIS

Moses led the people of God out of slavery, but he didn't get to lead them into the Promised Land. His journey was never about getting to that place; it was about faith. As the book of Hebrews helpfully points out about great people of faith, "They did not receive the things promised; they only saw them and welcomed them from a distance" (11:13). Moses' walk was a walk of faith, and at every turn he encountered hurdles. He refused to be known as the son of Pharaoh's daughter; he chose to be mistreated along with the people of God, rather than enjoy the pleasure of sin (Hebrews 11:24–26). He was disgraced and rejected, terrified and yet courageous. Even as the Lord began to speak to Moses, he was hitting hurdles in himself. The minute that we encounter God and consider stepping out of the boat, the obstacles may come thick and fast. How we respond to them affects who and what we become.

If only we could talk to him now and ask him if he would have chosen a different way, if he wished he had said a stronger "no" to the Lord, or if it was just too hard and not worth it. We wonder what his response would be. We doubt he would have chosen something else – not because he enjoyed all the hurdles he hit, but because he grew so close to God and saw Him move in incredible ways. We think Moses would say, as so many biblical leaders may too, that God is faithful and that the pain is worth the gain; that the "life in all its fullness" is indeed possible when we choose the will of God.

GOING TOGETHER

There were key things that enabled Moses to prepare for, endure, and overcome the hurdles that he had to face – tools he used to overcome them. The presence of Aaron, who was clearly called to walk alongside Moses, was no doubt a vital ingredient to his survival, as his sister's wise presence had also been when he was a tiny baby in the sea of reeds. The problem comes when we don't keep looking to God and to others, in order to overcome our hurdles; instead we think that we can handle things on our own. We heard a speaker talking recently and she painted a vivid view of our faith journey. She was referring to "Tough Mudder" – an endurance experience of going through ice cubes, climbing high walls, being electrocuted, getting caked in mud, etc. – intensely challenging and life changing. Although the course was run over many miles, it was not a race but about being a team, helping each other get to the finish. What seemed most profound was that "every time we got through one hurdle, we turned around to pull someone else through that obstacle too". She made it clear that this was a model for ministry on two levels: first, that we go through challenges and then lead someone else through a similar one, and second that we look at who has gone before and allow them to help us overcome the hurdle. **We serve alongside many others in the here and now but we also stand on the shoulders of the giants who have come before**.

We need each other. We have a great cloud of witnesses to help us run the race (Hebrews 12:1–2), but we also need people partnering with us in it. Sometimes the hurdles will be so great and overwhelming that we cannot see a way through, but Jesus sends us help. We need to face up to our hurdles alongside others, standing strong with one another.

From the very beginning of Moses' life the narrative is fascinating. We know without reading very far along that his start in life must signal an interesting journey ahead. It is here that we want to focus our attention for a moment: Moses was rescued from death, so that he could rescue others from death – that much we can acknowledge with hindsight. He was liberated that he too might liberate his people. The Exodus story is one of a great liberation and Moses is a huge driver in this. He was facing obstacles from the moment he was born but none of these was bigger or greater than the God he served.

Within the circumstances of the birth, the role of Moses' mother is interesting. Here was a woman who, when faced with a huge hurdle of potentially losing her child, was prepared to do a few things differently. Let's look at what she did when things got tough.

FACING THE HURDLE

Firstly, Moses' mother did something different from everyone else. Instead of being overwhelmed by Pharaoh's order to throw baby boys into the Nile – rather than letting that happen to her son – she acted. She was prepared to go against the rule of the day, to hide her child for three months, to prepare a basket perfectly to keep her child safe and hide it in the reeds along the Nile. Moses' mother confronted the problem in front of her, rather than letting it overwhelm her. She had wisdom in the face of adversity and responded incredibly. No wonder Moses was great: his mother was a genius! She could have given in to the order, seen her son die, and been overwhelmed with grief, but she found strength to do something different.

So often we can find ourselves faced with what feels like a mammoth task and no way through. We can give in to the problem and then fall into a greater mess, or we can speak to the mountain and ask it to move. We can seek clarity from the Lord, and He will always provide a way to stand up under it, to go through it, and to come out the other side. We feel like there is no way forward but Jesus sheds light onto situations so that we can see another way. Moses' mother had no idea what would happen to her son, but there was a way through and that way led to her being able to nurse him freely as she was intended to do. God has plans for us that sometimes don't make sense, but when He opens up the way, we begin to see why.

Fear so often cripples us into a place of not being able to move. The Hebrew mothers must have been so afraid about giving birth, wondering if it would be a boy and be thrown into the Nile. Rather than rejoicing in the pregnancy and new baby, the women would have been consumed with fear. When we think about how they must have felt, we are even more astounded that Moses' mum is able to do what she does. She finds a way, not to stop being afraid, but to not let it control what she does or stop her seeing another way. We love Nelson Mandela's quote when he says, "I learned that courage was not the absence of fear, but the triumph over it. **The brave man is not he who does not feel afraid, but he who conquers that fear.**"

There is a remarkable woman who comes along to our church's women's ministry each week for breakfast and a chat. The reason she began coming was because of horrendous circumstances. She had got to thirty-seven weeks in her pregnancy and the baby's heart stopped beating. This incredible woman had to give birth to her baby even though it was dead. As you might well imagine it has been a long journey of pain for her and the family, and we have done the best we can to support and pray particularly for her. Just recently she became pregnant again and is facing a situation that in our minds is similar to the plight of the Hebrew women: she does not know if this baby will live or die. The result of the last traumatic birth has left her riddled with fear and paranoia and the rest of us asking how we can help her to see a way through. We know that the fear is really unavoidable but what we are praying is that she will know peace beyond her understanding as she walks this journey, and that she can keep going and end up with a living healthy baby in her arms. Our bigger prayer is that through this she will meet Jesus and know that there is someone greater carrying her through this pregnancy – a God that she might learn to turn to no matter what she faces. We long that this precious lady can find a perspective of hope, even when all she knows is a picture of death – just like Moses' mother did.

SEEING DIFFERENTLY

Secondly, Moses' mother saw something in her son that was different from every other child: "When she saw that he was a fine child, she hid him for three months" (Exodus 2:2). She didn't see a baby boy that was destined for death; she saw the hand of God on his life. She saw a future and she had hope for Moses.

Sometimes we lose sight of God. We assume that what we hear and see is reality, and yet the Lord longs for us to allow His Holy Spirit to change our perspective. You could argue that there was no hope for Moses: Pharaoh was trying whatever he could to put Hebrew boys to death and Moses was one of them. Death, destruction, and decay can be staring us in the face but Jesus wants us to see differently. He longs that we might put on different lenses to see the situation as He sees it.

What God sees is not what we see; however, "God has chosen to make known among the Gentiles the glorious riches of this mystery, which is **Christ in you, the hope of glory**" (Colossians 1:27), and if this is the case then we need to ask Him to see more of what He sees! If we have Christ living in us then we can believe for so much more than what humanity presents to us. Having faith is so often hard but remains vital. None of this is rocket science; it begins and ends with prayers from the heart: "God, let me see this differently" and "God, give me faith to keep holding on and believing for more."

Sometimes our greatest challenges can actually turn out so very differently in the end. Ivy Blair works for the wonderful ministry Prospects (www.prospects.org.uk). Around the UK there are 200 Prospects ministry groups where, month by month, more than 3,000 people with learning disabilities meet together to worship God. For Ivy, her experiences having a child changed everything. Here's her story.

A new baby on the way – exciting or what? Then my son was born with Down's Syndrome in the days before screening and testing – no warning – he just arrived! Those first few days and weeks were bleak and tearful. Plans for the future – for him, for me as his mum, and family life – altered dramatically, and it did not seem a good change.

But God had a plan. That wee baby came as a teacher, to show his family and all those around them the true values in life – living in the moment, love without conditions, patience, a simple faith and lots of joy – and many times when my heart was sore and still is as problems in adulthood come along.

Having Neil changed my life dramatically. His faith journey has inspired me to share the good news of Jesus with other people with learning disabilities – and they have taught me so much about what a relationship with our friend Jesus is all about.

Ivy's incredible testimony is a challenge to us all to see things differently, to allow our circumstances and challenges to be used for good. Both she and Neil clearly have the DNA of game changers!

SURRENDER

Thirdly, the mother of Moses was prepared to give up her son so that he might live. This is just an absolutely breath-taking picture of the heart of the gospel: that the son would lay down His life so that we might live! Moses would not have to die like Jesus, but his life was laid down by his mother, ultimately to save the lives of God's people. This incredible woman was able to act differently to her peers by being willing to surrender something so precious to her, in the hope that he might live.

We cannot ignore this metaphor in Scripture; we have seen it previously with Abraham and Isaac, a father willing to lay down his son in obedience to God, so that God's promises could be fulfilled. Throughout the biblical narrative we see and hear a story of surrender, of holding things lightly, of being willing to hold loosely that which is most precious to us.

This picture of sacrifice, modelled ultimately in Christ's death on the cross, seems to be the most challenging image for our Western mindsets to grasp. In a world of uncertainty, we hold as tightly as we can to the things that are precious to us. In a society of individualism, where we seek to satisfy ourselves first, in communities of rights and privileges, the very notion of surrender creates a huge, thick wall of anxiety, stubbornness, and pride that we need to batter down. We also find that common sense in our minds kicks in, the protector and controller rises higher in our hearts than faith, and fear of what could be keeps us on the same safe journey that we think will be the best for us. The idea that we would come face to face with a huge hurdle and be willing to give up what seems important or significant to us, in order to see a breakthrough, is like a foreign language.

However, with the Spirit of God we can surrender anything; it is not something that we have to fight to do alone. In the last year we have seen a dramatic change in some of our friends. Since hearing God speak to them through the Acts of the Apostles, their whole worldview on finances and possessions has been transformed. In the past their outlook was similar to that of many middle-class Christians: we will have healthy children, move into a bigger house, get a nice car to accommodate us all, earn enough money to go on nice holidays, and be happy and comfortable. If anything isn't as we want it, then we will look to change it to accommodate our needs. And then something began to change. What was always a desire to help people outside of themselves has grown into them giving away more money than they would ever have dreamt. Through Scripture verses, specifically in Acts, and through others' prayers, they have been heavily immersed in a ministry that gives away clothes, food, shoes, furniture, and more. In the last eight months alone they have bought and done up three properties, enabling three families to move out of their inadequate living situations into homes that are suitable for them. The car that was bought to service the family's needs is now constantly full of furniture being delivered to needy families all over the community. Interestingly, all of these changes sound external, but the reality is that Jesus, by the power of the Holy Spirit, got hold of them internally first, through dynamic encounter, and that has led their lives, and the lives of many, to be transformed. Their view of finances is completely alien to what it was before. They believe with everything in them that nothing they have is theirs – it all belongs to God – and they could give it all away, but God will still always provide, no matter what they need. They have witnessed this time and again: as they have emptied their bank account, God has, in His mercy, replaced every penny. And what has this done to their faith? It makes them believe that they can move mountains. It gives them greater confidence, not in themselves, but in Christ.

When we think about our friends we are amazed at what God has done in and through them and how much it has challenged us. But the thing that we love the most is that they would not rather live the life that they had before, although the enemy may try to persuade them that it was better; they are free, they are liberated, they are living a life of surrender and seeing God come through.

This didn't happen overnight – there was a process of change in them. A small seed of faith grew into something greater. When God looks at us He takes us where we are and asks us, "Are we willing to lay down our lives for Him?" There are some things that God wants us to leave behind because they are actually useless to us and will not help us to climb the next mountain. These things may still feel important, but that is because they are familiar, comfortable, and make us feel good about ourselves. If we don't let go of them, we will have to carry them with us and then there will be too much on our plate to carry.

KEEP GOING

We sometimes simply need to keep going. Often it can feel like we expect life to be easy, for the path to be simple, for nothing to get in the way. It's as if we expect life to be a Disney Princess film in which all is wonderful and sugar-coated and we live happily ever after. Experience has certainly proved this not to be the case. We will find obstacles, problems, and hurdles; when facing these we need to keep moving. For anyone who has been pushed to their physical limits, the biggest challenge is to keep going and not give up.

The legendary basketball player Michael Jordan, who inspired millions worldwide to take up the game and/or wear his Nike-branded trainers, puts it this way: "If you're trying to achieve, there will be roadblocks. I've had them; everybody has had them. But obstacles don't have to stop you. **If you run into a wall, don't turn around and give up. Figure out how to climb it, go through it, or work around it.**"[1] As the stumbling blocks come along let's be people who aren't tripped over but who keep going. Let's find a way around, over, under or through the blocks!

American film producer George Lucas is the genius behind both *Indiana Jones* and *Star Wars*. He says:

You have to find something that you love enough to be able to take those risks, to be able to jump over the hurdles, to be able to break through the brick walls that are always going to be placed in front of you. You're not going to get anywhere without working extremely hard… You simply have to put one foot in front of the other and keep going. Put blinders on and plot right ahead.[2]

We want to be part of a church that loves Jesus enough to do the same!

Maybe things are really difficult for you right now and there are obstacles around you that seem insurmountable. Whatever our outlook it's important that we hold on to Jesus, live for Him, get over the hurdles, keep going, and last the pace. **He never promised it would be easy; He promised He'd always be with us**.

So keep going, simply putting one foot in front of the other and staying close to Jesus.

YES! But how?

YOU AND GOD

Consider where you are now. How do you feel about it? Is this the thing that God is calling you to? If you don't know what else it is, then it's probably where you are now. Can you see how God is calling you in it? If it's somewhere else, make a list of the things that need to change.

One of the hardest prayers to pray and really mean is quite possibly this:

> *"Lord, I will do whatever, go wherever, whenever you tell me to go!"*

- Can you pray it?
- Is there one aspect that is too hard for you?
- Why?
- Do you want to change where you stand on this?

Why not share your thoughts with someone you trust. Ask them how they feel about "wherever, whenever, whatever"; pray for one another for a deeper encounter with Christ and desire to do what He wants for you.

If you have time, listen to "Oceans", by Hillsong United, from the album *Zion*. (You may be able to access this online.)

Now try singing the chorus!
May you join Jesus on the waters.

GROUP ACTIVITY

1. Why not use the optical illusion of the woman who looks young to some and old to others below:

Ask the group to tell you what they see first – the old lady or the young one? Who sees the young woman the most? The old woman? Point out on the picture the features of both. Tell the group about Moses' mother (from the chapter) and her different perspective from the other Hebrew mothers on the birth of her son. Explain how sometimes our perspective stops us from seeing a much bigger picture of hope. Ask them to think of something that is worrying them. Pray that God might enlarge and change their perspective to see things differently.

2. Ask the group if they are "too comfortable, too safe or too popular?!" What is their response? Do they look for comfort, safety, and popularity? Why? Do they believe

that is what God has for them? Discuss. Is it time to make some uncomfortable decisions? Do you need to challenge one another? Read Isaiah 54:2 and ask them, "Is it time to 'Enlarge the place of your tent, stretch your tent curtains wide, do not hold back; lengthen your cords, strengthen your stakes'?" Pray for one another.

Further reading

G. Calver, A. Calver, *Stumbling Blocks* (Oxford: Monarch Books, 2012)
P. Regan, *When Faith Gets Shaken* (Oxford: Monarch Books, 2014)

6
Speak Up, Stand Up, Act Up

"In every generation, the world is changed by a few people, who stand for something, do not fear unpopularity and dare to make a difference."

NICKY GUMBEL

As a thirteen-year-old Gavin never really loved going to church. He would find himself sitting there every Sunday morning counting down the time till the service would finally finish and he'd be free from his Christian captivity. It's not that he was anti anything in particular at that stage; he just constantly yearned that there must be more to life than what was going on around him. People were singing with seemingly as little passion and intent as possible, the preacher always went on far too long, and at the end of church his mum would always be the last to leave once she'd finally finished chatting to every person in the room. That Christianity must be more than this strange Sunday morning gathering was what his thirteen-year-old self kept thinking. Surely this sanitized form of faith was not what Christianity was all about? He was used to standing on the terraces on a Saturday watching his beloved Wimbledon FC surrounded by people of passion, intent, and hope screaming their adulation. Why did church seem the opposite in terms of passion?

In truth Gavin's immaturity exaggerated the reality, but there still had to be more than this "Churchianity" that he found so boring. After all, Christianity is about living a sold-out life for Christ, and what he was encountering seemed so very far from that. He wanted to be part of a church on the move, making an impact – a remnant who were movers not settlers and were open to the leading of the Spirit at any point. Gavin's dad puts it this way: "The church is the company of believers, born again, yielded under the Lordship of Christ Jesus and living in a vital relationship with Him by the Holy Spirit. The church is the name of a family group called for a purpose, travelling to a specific destination to fulfil a glorious role in an eternity of ruling and reigning with her bridegroom."[1] Now that's more like it!

As a teenager Gavin wanted an adventure, not an average social club. **The church must never be a society but a radical remnant chasing after Jesus.** The Christian life is not a systematic set of problems and rules but something so much more exciting than that. John Eldridge puts it this way in his book *Wild at Heart*:

> Life is not a problem to be solved; it is an adventure to be lived. That's the nature of it and has been since the beginning when God set the dangerous stage for this high-stakes drama and called the whole wild enterprise good. He rigged the world in such a way that it only works when we embrace risk as the theme of our lives, which is to say, only when we live by faith.[2]

Somewhere along the journey of the UK church, everything appears to have become a bit too safe. We dream of Christians being liberated to fully live this adventure, to know the high-stakes nature of life, and to live with greater faith. We dream of a wild bunch who make the most of their opportunities, live on the edge, and show what it is to put faith in Jesus above everything else in the world; a renewed breed of Christians who are so dramatically changed by an encounter with the living Jesus that those around can't help but be transformed as well. Let's fight the temptation to reduce our Christian adventure to simply Sunday church attendance. There must be more!

One immediate problem in all of this is that many of us will question what we can do or what difference we might make within such a church. Yet here the example of Moses is incredible. He is someone who doubts himself, feels entirely inadequate, has killed someone, and is in exile; yet the Lord uses him to see incredible cultural transformation in his day. How then might the Lord want to use us today to do the same? What would it look like for the UK church to only ever gather in order that they might then be scattered, and to take more seriously its mandate to "go and make disciples" (Matthew 28:19)? We think the first thing needed is a move away from half-hearted Christianity. The West and apathy often seem to go hand in hand and we believe that we need to break out of this. **There's so much talk around how to achieve church growth and yet what is really needed are healthy Christians**. Healthy things grow and we need to focus on the health of our walk with Christ in order to be the game changers we desire to be.

Around the world right now are many Christians who are suffering incredibly for their faith. Christianity is seemingly being largely wiped out in the Middle East, and many have to stand up for their faith even if it costs them everything. The refugee crisis has further compounded this difficult landscape, with so many people being displaced. As we sit here writing in our dining room, such a reality feels – and is – half a world away. But how can we raise our game here, have our faith central to everything, and change the world? Inspired by all that Moses did in confronting Pharaoh we can't help but think that we need to get a bit more stuck in. We need to rise up and make an impact in our community. Yes! But how?

A BIBLICAL EXAMPLE

A particular hero of ours in the Bible is a little known guy called Epaphroditus. He's a consummate unsung hero and one that we've enjoyed preaching on over the years. He's only mentioned for six verses in the entire Bible and these can be found in Philippians 2:25–30. Coming straight off the back of the great and famous hymn of the early church at the start of Philippians 2, it appears on a first reading that Paul is getting a little sidetracked in mentioning him at all. However, this is not the case, as all Paul is saying is that Epaphroditus (and indeed Timothy) are living examples of those who have put into practice the words of the hymn. They are doing their best to live out the truths they sing in the world around them. This is particularly important in today's culture, where we can be in danger of going from one Christian bless up to another without ever fully putting what we've sung and learnt into practice. As Christians we must do all we can to put our Christian experiences and encounters into practice by then living differently in our world. Our faith and worship must both have "legs" and be lived out in our environment. **We show how different we are when amongst those who don't know Christ, not when locked away in church!**

The nature of his commitment is also hugely counter-cultural. Epaphroditus is "especially worthy of honour because of his self-sacrificing devotion to the work of

Christ".[3] In our world of consumerism and looking after number one, a figure who is prepared to put down his own agenda and give everything over to God provides quite a challenge to the rest of us. We know ourselves that we're constantly in danger of falling into the trap of wanting to know what we might get out of something. That is totally the wrong approach and we should emulate Epaphroditus in laying down our agenda and getting onto God's. After all, Jesus says in Matthew 16:24–26: "Whoever wants to be my disciple must deny themselves and take up their cross and follow me. For whoever wants to save their life will lose it, but whoever loses their life for me will find it."

Despite only appearing in six verses of Scripture Epaphroditus is described by many theologians, such as Warren Wiersbe, as a "balanced Christian".[4] This is an intriguing accolade and manifests itself in his life in four distinct ways: he's faithful as a brother, is a messenger, and a servant (verse 25). Most importantly for us, though, is the fourth thing he is – a risk taker (verse 30). The Greek verb *paraboleumai* occurs only here in the New Testament as it describes Epaphroditus' risk taking. Elsewhere in the culture it was used as a gambling term, as is explained below. In essence the idea of the word is that you are prepared to put everything on the table, to go "all in" and risk all you have and are. Alec Motyer puts it this way: "He took a calculated risk, involving the expenditure of all he had, relying only on the trustworthiness of Jesus Christ. He staked all on Jesus, knowing that He could not fail."[5] This incredible example then inspired others to do the same. Gordon Fee points out that Epaphroditus serves as a model of one who was willing to suffer for the sake of Christ and that we must not be afraid to do the same if necessary.[6] We too must be prepared to risk absolutely everything for the sake of Christ.

In the early church there was a group of people who called themselves the "Parabolani". Coming from the same Greek word *paraboleumai*, it is best translated in English as "to risk", "to hazard", or "to gamble". As a result the Parabolani were often called the "reckless ones". They were men and women who risked themselves for the sake of Christ. They formed a group, agreeing together to move into any place of danger or risk, to serve and help others. Whenever anyone was sick with a dangerous disease, they would go and minister to them. When they learned of men who were in dungeons, dangerous criminals, they would risk their lives to help them, to do something for them. They would send evangelists into leper colonies, because how else would lepers hear the gospel? In reality this would be a death sentence for the individuals involved because they would not be allowed out of the leper colony once they had gone in. This group became infamous for their risky approach to life and the fact they would go anywhere to share Christ, whatever the price tag.

In AD 252 the great city of Carthage, North Africa, was hit by a plague sweeping through the city with such ferocity that it left total devastation in its wake. Bodies piled up and no one was prepared to bury them for fear of catching the deadly disease. The sun pounded down on the dead bodies, and this, coupled with animals transferring it, did nothing but amplify the problem of the plague. The scene grew bleaker and bleaker. The city was standing on the precipice of total ruin.

The then Bishop of Carthage, Cyprian, cried out for the Parabolani to help his city. He also challenged the local Christians to become the Parabolani in their own community. This battle cry was responded to positively, and the Parabolani swept into Carthage en masse, burying the bodies in the name of Jesus and telling anyone that would listen why they were doing it. As a result two very significant things happened.

First, the city of Carthage was saved and the plague was stopped in its tracks. Second, one of the most incredible and significant revivals in the early church took place in Carthage. When Christians live their faith, speak their faith, and act out their faith, the world can't help but be affected in a profound way. Actions and words together change the world.

This group of Christians became an incredible example of living out Christianity and reaching those everyone else had given up on. The church leader Malcolm Duncan puts it this way: "The Parabolani became a movement that served the broken, the poor, the forgotten and the vulnerable. Inspired by the example of Epaphroditus, they too gave up the security of what they knew and embarked on the adventure of a lifetime as they served those whom others rejected."[7]

WHAT ABOUT US?

So what does this all mean now? **Where are the Parabolani of our day?** Where are those who will expend themselves for the cause of Jesus Christ? Surely that is God's call on us today, to put it all on the line for Him? All around the world there are examples of people doing just that. In recent times the rapid uprising of the so-called Islamic State has put huge pressure on Christians in the Middle East. Christians have often been given a simple and stark choice: recanting their faith and turning to radical Islam, or being put to death. In the face of such a horrible reality many Christians have boldly stood up for Jesus. Hearing so many stories of Christians losing their lives as a result of this choice has been devastating, heartbreaking, and yet also inspiring, as people stick by the courage of their convictions. Our desperate prayer in the middle of such tragedy is that – as the case has so often been throughout church history – the challenges and pain so many

Christians face lead to significant growth for the church.

In March 2015 there was one particularly graphic moment when twenty-one Egyptian Coptic Christians were beheaded on a beach by their IS captors stood behind them. As the men's heads were cut off they could be heard proclaiming Christ and His kingship. One of IS's primary motivations for this act was to start a war between moderate Christians and Muslims in Egypt. However, the Bible Society in Cairo responded differently and instead chose to forgive. They produced a tract full of Scripture, which had the following poem on the back:

> *Two rows of men walked the shore of the sea,*
> *On a day when the world's tears would run free,*
> *One a row of assassins, who thought they did right,*
> *The other of innocents, true sons of the light,*
> *One holding knives in hands held high,*
> *The other with hands empty, defenceless and tied,*
> *One row of slits to conceal glaring-dead eyes,*
> *The other with living eyes raised to the skies,*
> *One row stood steady, pall-bearers of death,*
> *The other knelt ready, welcoming heaven's breath,*
> *One row spewed wretched, contemptible threats,*
> *The other spread God-given peace and rest.*
>
> *A Question...*
>
> *Who fears the other?*
> *The row in orange, watching paradise open?*
> *Or the row in black, with minds evil and broken?*[8]

What an incredible response. What could be a more profound way to respond to such barbaric acts of violence and persecution than to offer the olive branch of forgiveness? Those Christians going to heaven sooner than planned at no point lost hope in where they were headed and the overwhelming presence of God. **The Christian life was never supposed to be easy and may cost us everything, but in the end the cost is dwarfed by what Christ has done for us and the life He brings**. What an example of a postmodern Parabolani the Egyptian church is in this instance. Their words have been powerful, but coupled with their actions in not retaliating, the words are amplified yet further.

Bringing things closer to home once more, how can we in the UK bring more of ourselves to Christ as "living sacrifices" (Romans 12:1)? How can we live all out for Jesus? For a start we need to be prepared to give Him everything and to see this for what it is. Everything we have and are is God-given, so anything we give back is simply returning to the Lord that which is already His. C. S. Lewis puts it this way:

> *Every faculty you have, your power of thinking or of moving your limbs from moment to moment, is given you by God. If you devoted every moment of your whole life exclusively to His service you could not give Him anything that was not in a sense His own already. So that when we talk of a man doing anything for God or giving anything to God, I will tell you what that is really like. It is like a small child going to its father and saying, "Daddy, give me sixpence to buy you a birthday present."*[9]

We need to return to God that which is His – us.

IT IS POSSIBLE

Why then would we not return to the Lord that which is already His? Looking around the UK there are some incredible examples of people speaking up, standing up, and acting up for

Christ with all they have. One is Christians Against Poverty (CAP). John Kirkby, the Founder and International Director of CAP, says this, reflecting on what's been achieved thus far:

> I am overwhelmed by what God has done. To see thousands of lives changed every year is truly wonderful. I do believe that God has given us a 21st Century answer to one of the most pressing social needs within society today. Jesus met people's needs with love, compassion and practical help. Our desire is to simply do the same and watch the miracles unfold.[10]

CAP is a wonderful example of words and deeds together, of bringing hope practically and yet also offering a rescue to people spiritually too. It is also further evidence that in order to impact our nation we sometimes need to get out of the church and into our communities. We will usually need to reach people on their turf, not ours.

Such stories are inspiring and they are not isolated. Throughout the UK we are seeing Christians rolling up their sleeves and getting involved in kingdom work. The growth of the Hope ministry these past few years has been evidence of Christians taking seriously a holistic approach to mission, encompassing both essential elements of word and deed. Equally, our fourteen years in Youth for Christ exposed us to many examples of Christians making an impact. Most astounding to us was the impact we had on prisoners in custody, as young people who'd never known true hope finally found eternal hope in a relationship with Jesus. Once they were out of custody these young people were some of the most incredible evangelists we've ever come across. They knew what it was to be saved and were desperate to reach their communities. A little like the Samaritan woman in John 4, these young people experienced grace in a profound way, which led them to wanting to bring their whole village to Jesus too.

So what does this all mean for us? Well, for a start, who does no one love in your community? What could you do to bring Christ's love to them? In what areas could you step up for Christ and begin to take your mission for Him more seriously? Christianity has been built on people who've been prepared to take risks, give everything, and go out on a limb for God. From Noah to William Wilberforce, Esther to Corrie ten Boom, and Peter the disciple to Martin Luther King, Jr we have the opportunity to stand on the shoulders of giants. Let's be a postmodern Parabolani going all in for Christ. As the missionary Jim Elliot, who was eventually killed by the Auca Indians he went to reach, famously once said, "He is no fool who gives what he cannot keep to gain what he cannot lose." Let's not hold on to the temporary over that which is eternal!

It's not all about massive impact on a huge scale either. Sometimes we start simply by trying to bring about the common good and a piece of kingdom where we are. There was a lady who worked in what was known as the "corner from hell" in her office. Everyone was horrible to each other in that part of the building, and backbiting and gossip were rife. This lady was a Christian and she wanted things to be different so she decided to change things. She started to pray for her colleagues and performed acts of kindness: on anyone's birthday she brought in cakes, she did jobs for others, made drinks, and spoke well of everyone. Soon enough it became the best corner of the office and everyone's behaviour changed because **one game changer went against the status quo in the name of Jesus.** In another situation some of our closest friends have long-term fostered a lovely little girl with all manner of additional needs. This girl had faced intolerable cruelty in her previous environment and now, as a result of our friends' compassion and kindness, her world is being turned around. These friends of ours have allowed their love for Christ to be poured out on someone who otherwise may never have experienced this. Both of these instances are wonderful demonstrations of the love of Christ and evidence that we can change the world one person at a time.

What might you be able to do in your environment? More widely, what about your town? Research from the Cinnamon Network shows that faith groups (with the overwhelming majority being Christian) provide over £3 billion worth of support and people hours into changing society.[11] This is an incredible figure, but what might you be able to do alongside other Christians and churches in your town to make a difference?

This life is short and we only get one shot at it. Let's be the kind of people that risk everything for the worthiness of Christ. Like Epaphroditus let's make a calculated decision to expend all we have, and are, for the sake of God. Let's be balanced Christians who are faithful, who carry a message, who serve others, and who take risks. What's stopping us? The biggest answer to that is probably fear. Fear of what others think, of being ostracized, of offending people, of not fitting in, of it costing us too much, of being rejected, of setting the bar too high, of rocking the boat too much, of being counter-cultural, of losing our credibility, of standing out too much. Sounds a little like all Christ risked for us, to be fair! Let's pray that Christ is with us and that our fears don't cripple us. We want to see the nation changed, and as a famous quote says, **"Don't let your fears stand in the way of your dreams."**[12]

YES! But how?

YOU AND GOD

What is the Lord asking of you?

Speak Up: Is the Lord Jesus encouraging you to find a way to speak up about what you believe and whom you believe in? Perhaps you are socially engaged in the work of the Lord but struggle to accredit it to Him? There is power in the name of Jesus! Try using His name in conversation this week.

Stand Up: Perhaps there is an issue that you see in the church or outside of it that really makes you frustrated… You can't understand why you feel so strongly about it and yet no one else is beating the same drum. The Lord often stirs our hearts with the things that are stirring His. If you feel the unease, don't pass the buck or the complaint to someone else: you could be the answer!

Act Up: Have you taken action over the things that are on your heart? There is always a reason why it is "not a good time" to attempt something. Who knows what will happen tomorrow. If you feel the passion, act now.

GROUP ACTIVITY

Biblical reflection

1. **Stephen's speech to the Sanhedrin (Acts 7:1–60)** Stephen spoke up for God and he ended up losing his life for the sake of his faith. Why not read this chapter as a group, all the way through, asking God how, where, and in what way you can speak up more boldly in the name of Jesus? Discuss together.

2. **Epaphroditus (Philippians 2:25–30)** Epaphroditus was a balanced Christian. He was faithful, a messenger, a servant, and a risk taker. Maybe spend some time reflecting on this man and asking yourself, are you out of balance? Is there an area that you can ask God to grow in your life? Remember: healthy things grow! Identify the areas in which you struggle and pray for one another for strength.

Some ministries that can help you make a difference:

A Rocha – The gospel is good news for the whole of creation, as well as for human beings. A Rocha UK equips the church to demonstrate this good news for God's earth.
More info at: www.arocha.org.uk/resources/

The **Bible Society** makes Scriptures available where there are none. It works to help the church engage with the Bible more effectively. And it endeavours – through the arts, education, media, and politics – to make the Bible available, accessible, and credible in our culture.
More info at: www.biblesociety.org.uk

Christians Against Poverty (CAP) enables people to get out of poverty, working through the local church to provide debt counselling, money courses, job clubs and more, without compromising on sharing the gospel.
More info at: www.capuk.org

Care for the Family supports anyone in all areas of family life, such as marriage, parenting, bereavement, and single parenting.
More info at: www.careforthefamily.org.uk

Cinnamon works to bring together people in need in communities, with people and resources from local churches. More info at: www.cinnamonnetwork.co.uk

The **Church Mission Society** (CMS) are people in mission who want the world to know Jesus: a mission community living a mission lifestyle and supporting Christian mission worldwide.
Find out more at:www.cms-uk.org/

The Evangelical Alliance is passionate about resourcing and equipping the church to build unity, do mission, develop leaders, and keep up to date with the latest developments in the Christian world.
More info at: www.eauk.org/church/resources/

Hope is a catalyst for local church mission in villages, towns, and cities, with resources and practical ways to reach out in word and deed together.
See: www.hopetogether.org.uk

The **London Institute of Contemporary Christianity** (LICC) equips Christians and churches for whole-life discipleship, wherever you find yourself engaging in the world.
More info at: www.licc.org.uk

Open Doors is an international ministry serving persecuted Christians and churches worldwide that seeks to mobilize the church in the UK and Ireland to serve Christians living under religious persecution. Visit: www.opendoorsuk.org

Redeeming Our Communities (ROC) wants to form partnerships with agencies, groups, and churches to bring about community transformation.
See: www.roc.uk.com

Street Pastors engage with people on the streets to care for them, listen to them, and help them. They work together with other partners in the night-time economy to make communities safer.
Visit: www.streetpastors.org

Tearfund is a leading relief and development charity. Tearfund works in partnership with Christian agencies and churches worldwide to tackle the causes and effects of poverty.
More info at: www.tearfund.org

Part 3

EVERYONE

Exodus 17:8–15

7
It Takes All of Us

"If you want to go fast, go alone. If you want to go far, go together."

AFRICAN PROVERB

Let's picture the scene at Rephidim in Exodus 17:8–16: we find a weary tribe of God's people who have encountered all kinds of challenges to lead them to this point. They have lived as oppressed slaves, had to run in fear from their enemy, felt desperation in the desert – all undergirded with a deep nomadic lack of stability and security. Now here they are with another battle to face – to beat the Amalekites and press on towards the Promised Land. The Israelites must have learnt so much about their Lord and about themselves through this journey, but now He has something important and new to teach and to show them. Instead of fighting *for* His children, their King is going to work *through* them.

Sometimes the Lord will do incredible miraculous things for us and we can sit back in wonder, marvelling at the way He has moved in power. We should celebrate such instances, have faith for them, and continue to pray that it might be so. However, we need to be open to God operating through us as well. God's ways are not our ways and we cannot expect Him to work in the same manner. He is creative and full of surprises.

Our culture teaches us to expect things instantly and on our terms, but the benefit of spiritual hindsight so often shows how the Lord was working through us in a situation that in the end worked out for the best, even though we couldn't see it at the time.

So here are the Israelites getting reading for battle against the Amalekites – but who were this enemy that they had to face? Philip Hyatt describes them as "a wide-ranging desert tribe, or confederation of tribes, who are uniformly represented as enemies of Israel".[1] Additionally, they were nomads in the desert south of Canaan and descendants of Esau, who were attempting to remove the Israelites from this pleasant area so that they could have it and were also seeking to protect their own land from possible future intrusion.[2] They were enemies of the Israelites, who were seeking to hold their territory and kick Moses and his friends out.

So what was the plan for this battle? How were the Israelites going to overcome their enemy? The answer: through four distinct individuals. We can often misunderstand how things happen. Behind every success, victory or transformation are people. In our world of big brands, famous sports teams, and consumerism we could be forgiven for thinking that people bear no consequence to triumph, but this would be a totally wrong reading of things. The Scottish entrepreneur and founder of Kwik-Fit, Sir Tom Farmer, once said that **"organisations don't have success, people do"**. Behind any achievement, change or revolution will be a load of people making a difference, not just a sterile strategic plan. It's people that bring about transformation in the name of the Lord. That's why we can be the game changers that our culture requires. This battle with the Amalekites is no different. It's people that will change things.

So who are the four people involved on this occasion?

First, we've obviously got Moses, the central character of this book and a great leader who's used incredibly by the Lord. Second, we've got Joshua. This passage is the first mention of him in the Bible, but as we know from here, and later references, he's a victorious, Spirit-filled believer who's bold and obedient. Third, we have Aaron, who's already been appointed high priest. Finally, we have this other guy, Hur. But who on earth is he? We know almost nothing about him at all, yet he's mentioned in such good company. He was as essential to this victory as any of the big three he found himself serving with.

Joshua entered in with zeal and enthusiasm, and his work in battle didn't change very much throughout the day; however, he found that "as long as Moses held up his hands, the Israelites were winning, but whenever he lowered his hands, the Amalekites were winning" (verse 11). In the end the victory was secured in a unique fashion in order to demonstrate God's power. Moses holding the staff of God above his head with both hands symbolized Israel's total dependence on the power of God. When Moses lowered his hands, a picture of lack of dependence, the enemy was winning. With the assistance of Aaron and Hur, Moses' hands remained uplifted and a great victory was secured.[3] Moses was so thankful to have the other two there with him. The battle could not have been won without the assistance of Aaron and Hur holding up his arms. **They may not have had the prominent position but they were absolutely vital**.

This passage also teaches us about the fundamental value of prayer and action. Joshua is in the thick of the battle, but it is the prayers of Moses that bring about victory. Assisted by Aaron and Hur his prayers see the battle won but at the same time Joshua is still needed in the battle. Nonetheless **there's no disputing the fact that victory comes about not as a result of**

military muscle but supernatural intervention. Phil Moore puts it this way: "What mattered was not the strength of Israel's army but the strength of Israel's God, as Moses laid hold of his throne in prayer."[4] God comes through for the Israelites but He chooses to do so through using these four key figures.

LESSONS FROM HUR

Of all four characters in the story we are particularly interested in Hur. He's the one we relate to most. We won't all be heroes like Moses, warriors like Joshua or high priests like Aaron, but we can all play our part like Hur. We can all bring what little we can offer and ask God to work through it. We can all show up and make ourselves available. We find it massively encouraging that the Lord would use someone like Hur, as it shows us that He would also use people like you and me too. Looking more closely at this character, there are three things that we think are particularly important for us to learn from him.

First, people like Hur, though initially seeming insignificant, are absolutely invaluable in the Lord's service (verse 12). When Moses was growing tired, Hur (and Aaron) got a stone for him to sit on to ease the discomfort and held his hands up either side of him in order that Moses would remain steady all day. This was so vital, as every time Moses dropped his arms the momentum of the battle changed against Israel. Therefore, his arms had to stay up and the assistance of Hur in this made the victory possible. What a significant role Hur had. It wasn't the most publicly celebrated role, but nonetheless it was absolutely fundamental in achieving victory. Some people go unnoticed and un-thanked for most of their Christian lives, performing vital duties without recognition. We all know of incredible and humble servants of God who do so much without ever getting the kind of appreciation afforded to the worship leader or wealthy Christian businessman. This is the fault of our humanity in not recognizing everyone's contribution as being equal. All must play their part, and regardless of public praise all must still step up. Recognized or not, all are essential. If Hur (and Aaron) had not done what they did, Moses would have failed, and so would Joshua. Without Hur the battle's outcome would have been so different.

Second, people Like Hur are always involved in what's going on (verses 10, 12). We will find these people wherever the action is taking place. In the passage, Hur stole a lead on so many by actually going to the top of the hill in the first place! Once up there he did all that was practically needed to bring about victory. At no point is he a spectator or bystander. Hur rolls up his sleeves and gets involved. His role was different to others but he stepped up and did what was needed.

One of Gavin's best mates is a guy called Jon. They're very different and yet they've also got plenty in common. However, whilst Gavin's often doing things up front, Jon is the most faithful servant of God you could imagine. He doesn't always get the credit but he always gets involved. If any practical task needs doing he's the person for the job. If someone has overlooked something he'll quietly do it. We admire him more than most people we know, because instead of waiting for the headlines he simply gets involved and does what he can to bring about God's kingdom. He doesn't want praise and will be cross we've written this about him, but what he does is vital. In short he's a postmodern Hur.

Hur wasn't a wonderful leader like Moses, or a great general like Joshua. Nor had he been anointed like Aaron, yet he was involved in the Lord's work! Not everyone is called to lead. Not all Christians will get the same focus put on them during this life; not all will be anointed in the same way, but all must be involved. As people who are privileged to speak on quite a few platforms we thank the Lord for all those who make that possible. Many think the speaker is in charge but that's not true. The most powerful person in the room runs the sound desk. Without them doing their job there might as well be no talk!

We all need to be involved in the Lord's service, making ourselves available to do what is required. That may take us to places we never thought possible, or may not, but we must always be serving. We once heard a great talk in which the message was simple: if you're not sure what to do in service of Jesus just do what's in front of you. Simply get involved in making a difference right where you are. Don't wait for the Lord to shout through the clouds about a great anointing that's about to be bestowed upon you. Get involved here and now and He'll use you.

Third, people like Hur are often unseen (verse 12). You could go further still and say he's even invisible. Hur's not mentioned before this point in the Bible, and there's only one other mention of him later on (Exodus 24:14). He is not to be confused with two other Hurs mentioned (Exodus 31:2; 35:30; 38:22) and a Midianite king (Numbers 31:8; Joshua 13:21).[5] It's rumoured he's the husband of Miriam, Moses' sister, but theologian Alan Cole writes, "Jewish tradition is imaginative but valueless in making him out to be Miriam's husband."[6] Hur is largely unknown before, during, and after this moment in Israelite history.

Clearly this character spent his time out of the limelight. He lived in the shadows of others, invisible to those who looked up to Moses, Aaron, and Joshua. You can imagine too that after the battle was won against the Amalekites everyone would have congratulated Moses and Joshua massively and maybe Aaron too, but no one would have extended the same celebration and gratitude towards Hur. Yet we need people like Hur. To bring about any kind of change takes a diverse group of people, not just those everyone venerates. What was unseen by people was not missed by the Lord. While others failed to notice his efforts, God was thinking, "Well done, my good and faithful servant!"

Let's encourage those who faithfully serve the Lord, especially those who are involved in ways that are unseen and not publicly praised. We have witnessed so many folk thinking so negatively about themselves, partly because they serve behind the scenes. One of the dangers is that we compare ourselves and what we do with what others are seen to be doing, and then we conclude that our role is not worth anything compared to theirs. Hur was invaluable, but did anyone ever tell him? Yes, we need to know our worth in Christ, but everyone needs appreciating. Comparison will kill us and our ministry; let's keep focusing on Jesus and the call that He has placed on us – fulfilling that to the best of our ability.

WHAT ABOUT US?

Having grown up as the "son of a preacher man" and now having numerous ministry opportunities of his own, Gavin has seen first-hand how we sometimes celebrate certain gifts and personalities in the Christian world over others. This has got to stop. Nothing will change in Britain if we're dependent on the odd charismatic personality who can deliver a rousing talk. We need a mobilized church, with every person playing their part and stepping into all that the Lord has for them. We need to value each and every contribution, in the knowledge that we need one another and that together we are stronger. We need to be game changers everywhere, in each sphere of our society, with a value placed on all of this.

Throughout his life Gavin has always played in football teams. For years he was a goalkeeper, and after an injury involving his arms dislocating he has reimagined himself as a centre back. In truth, however, he's always wanted to be a striker. They get to score all the goals and play in the most celebrated position. Equally, if they make a mistake it doesn't usually cost their team a goal or even the result. They can quickly make up for a catalogue of missed chances with a single goal. Juxtaposed to this reality is his role in any football team he's played for. He has always had unglamorous roles – the ones that get the least praise and the most blame. As a goalie, even if Gavin's had a great game, blocking dozens of potential goals, one little mistake could easily cost his team the game, and he could find himself to be the most vilified team member.

A combination of a lack of ability and only playing in goal till he was nineteen meant that he would never be a striker in any team. The glory may not be his, but the collection of trophies and medals on his desk were won by him too. The strikers he's played with would not have won them without his efforts too. Gavin may have played football without the praise and glory but he still played his part, and as a result the team did well. In a similar way **we need to start seeing the church as a collective within which we all need to work together in order to change a nation**. It's not enough to leave it to a few. Whatever we have, whoever we know, we need to use our gifts to play our part, just like Hur did.

When God created us He never intended that we'd all be the same. Human beings have an awful lot in common with one another and yet are each profoundly unique. We are all made in the image of God (Genesis 1:27) and yet all created distinct. When God made you He threw the mould away, not because it was broken but because one of you is enough! If you get close to any human being you realize how amazing and special they are but you also realize that one of them is what is needed. We don't want clones of people; we want each person being comfortable in their humanity whilst embracing the uniqueness of their individuality.

For some of us we need to accept how special we are and how much the Lord delights in us (Zephaniah 3:17). For many years at Christian festivals young people would wear a t-shirt with the slogan, "When God made me He was showing off." Cheeky though this statement is, it's actually quite profound. We are the pinnacle of His creation and He thinks we're absolutely amazing. Like with Hur, He doesn't miss what you do, who you are, and all you bring. Even if the world may seem not to notice you, He sees it all. Even if we are more like Hur than Moses and will need to operate in the shadows, we must still bring what we have and let the Lord work through us. The eighteenth-century political theorist and philosopher Edmund Burke said, **"Nobody made a greater mistake than he who did nothing because he could only do a little."** Let's not be people who do nothing because it seems insignificant; let's be game changers who bring what seems to the world to be a little, and allow the Lord to use it immeasurably more than we could ask or imagine (Ephesians 3:20).

If we are going to see incredible change in this nation then it is going to take all of us playing our part. In its simplest form everyone must be involved. Regardless of the worth put on our role by the world, church or ourselves, we must be involved and active as together we are stronger. Perhaps for some of you reading this you long to be an Aaron or a Joshua and don't want to be a Hur. Maybe you find yourself as a Moses and long to be on the sidelines more. Whatever the reality, we need to find gratitude in who, and what, we are in order to then minister out of it.

Hard though it may be, we need to be able to say, like the psalmist, "I praise you because I am fearfully and wonderfully made; your works are wonderful, I know that full well" (Psalm 139:14). It's so easy to resent who we are and what we do; to long to be someone else and think it's so much better for others. But God made you to be yourself. Gavin wanted to be a striker but he's a centre back! Growing up in the church, there was one particular song we remember most vividly from our childhood because we love animals. Anyone of our age or older will probably be familiar with the song "If I were a butterfly". The song talks about what you would be grateful for if you were a different creature. However, the crux of the message is the chorus. It goes like this: "For you gave me a heart and you gave me a smile. You gave me Jesus and you made me your child. And I just thank you, Father, for making me, me."[7]

In order to serve Him fully and be the change this nation needs, we all need to embrace who we are and be grateful to God for making us that which He did. When He created you he didn't make a mistake. Other people may not help with this all the time. Gavin has spent most of his Christian ministry being compared to his Dad and yet he's not him. He's like him, but he's so grateful to God that he made him Gav – not Clive mark two, but Gav. We need to fight against the disease of comparison that helps no one and does nothing constructive within the kingdom. We are all unique and yet together we are all stronger. We need to pray that we can find ourselves in a place where we are grateful for that which we were made.

We need to step into who we are. Like Hur we need to be involved. What is there that you could be doing that you've previously not done? Where might the Lord want to use you in new and imaginative ways? How might you be more active for Him? We also need to acknowledge the truth that, like

Hur, we too are invaluable. It may not always feel like it, but what we do and who we are, are entirely unique and therefore fundamentally important. You are so special and so significant. Finally, we may need to accept, as Hur did, that all of this may well mean that at times we too seem invisible. Many may not notice, we may never be thanked or acknowledged, but the Lord sees everything and delights in you.

We can also take great encouragement from the fact that Christ is with us in it all, making our impact and our efforts go so very much further. The renowned biblical scholar Matthew Henry puts it this way: "Christ is both to us – our Joshua, the captain of our salvation who fights our battles, and our Moses, who, in the upper world, ever lives making intercession, that our faith fail not."[8] Far be it from us to correct Matthew Henry, but we would simply add that Christ is also our Hur and Aaron, supporting, refreshing, and renewing us when it is all too hard and we feel like giving in.

YES! But how?

YOU AND GOD

Who are you most like in this story? (Exodus 17:8–16)

- Do you identify with Hur?
- Whose arms are you called to hold up, or to pray for?
- Do you identify with Joshua?
- What battle are you called to fight?
- Do you identify with Moses?
- What direction are you called to set?
- Do you identify with Aaron?
- Whom are you called to partner with and speak for?

Maybe in some ways you identify with all of them!
Are you in particular danger of comparing yourself to others?

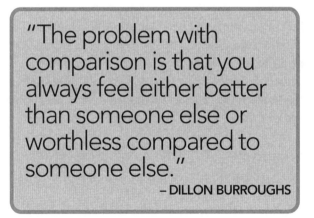

"The problem with comparison is that you always feel either better than someone else or worthless compared to someone else."
– DILLON BURROUGHS

God made you unique... Spend some time seeking His heart for how He sees you.

GROUP ACTIVITY

1. Take a look together at Exodus 17:8–16 and consider the characters. How many of the group feel a bit like Hur? Do they feel like what they are doing is not really noticed or valuable? Perhaps they have an unseen role and are rarely encouraged. Maybe they struggle with comparing themselves to others. Ask the "Hurs" to stand, then ask those around them to lift up their arms. Speak truth over them: they are children of God, who are called and valuable. Use Scripture to lift them up in their spirits and pray for them.

2. Moses had people in his life to help him with what the Lord was calling him to do. Emphasize the fact that He never calls us to minister without bringing the right people around us. Moses had Miriam, Aaron, Hur, Joshua. He had his father-in-law giving advice in crucial moments. Spend some time asking God together to show you who He is putting or has already put around you. Ask the Lord to show you what part they play and the gifts that they have. Discuss this with someone near you and see if they have thoughts to add or questions to ask. Even better, ask if they know who you are talking about! Pray that Jesus would connect relationships around callings in a deeper way.

Further reading

C. Madavan, *Digging for Diamonds* (Milton Keynes: Authentic Media, 2014)

M. Lucado, *You are Special* (Oxford: Candle Books, 2004)

8
Body Ministry

*"I can do things you cannot, you can do things I
cannot; together we can do great things."*

MOTHER TERESA

One of the craziest, or possibly stupidest, ideas Gavin ever had was to try to break the Guinness World Record for the longest ever five-a-side football match. The rules were really tight from Guinness, and alongside fifteen other players (there were two squads of eight, with five from each playing at any given time), Gavin attempted this on 30 April 2013. So many people contributed towards making this mega event a possibility. Over the twelve months prior to the event taking place there had been loads of meetings, with a big group working out the logistics. Once we were ready to start the attempt the whole thing had to be filmed, so there was a video team doing this. Food and drink, massages, medical expertise, blister plasters, and ice baths were all provided, and there were teams working on these too. Players were allowed to sleep for twenty minutes at a time, and there was a poor team tasked with waking up the exhausted footballers as well.

Further still, there were supporters to help the teams keep going, officials to keep score and note any yellow and red cards, and referees too. Then there were other less obvious tasks required, such as people stood behind the goals in the middle of the night with brooms to prod the goalkeepers and make sure they didn't fall asleep. The whole thing was a huge team effort, and though sixteen players took part, more than twice as many others were involved in the attempt in order for it to have a chance of success. At 10 a.m. on 2 May 2013 the final whistle went and the team had set a new World Record of playing five-a-side football for forty-eight hours, raising £53,000 for Youth for Christ in the process.

As Gavin gave a speech to all the people gathered on the pitch and the assembled media, there were so many people to thank. The attention was on the players, but they would not have broken any record without the huge team who all worked together in many different roles towards the same end. It's incredible what is possible when people play to their strengths, work hard to help each other, operate in a clearly united way, and pursue a common outcome with clear focus. Former President of the USA Harry S. Truman said, **"It is amazing what you can accomplish if you do not care who gets the credit."** How much might be possible if we all work as one body and not one of us gets the credit, because God gets it all.

None of us can, or were intended to, do it all alone. The Moses narrative shows us that it was impossible for him to manage the work of God in solitude. He needed many people – some that are named, some that are not – to enable him to lead the people where the Lord was calling them to go. Jethro, Joshua, Aaron, Caleb, Hur, and Miriam are just a few examples of the people that partnered with Moses to lead the children of God towards the Promised Land.

BEING ONE

We find it impossible to talk about the work of God without acknowledging the vital need for us to "be one". Even the God that we follow is part of a "Godhead", with the Father, Son and Holy Spirit deeply and intimately connected yet reflecting different aspects of our Lord.

We cannot engage in mission without rereading the words from John 17, where Jesus explicitly focuses on the need for unity as He prays for the disciples and for all those who will believe through His message (17:6–26). When Jesus prays for protection for the disciples, He is praying that they might be "one as we are one" (17:11) – as one like the Godhead, in order to reflect the Lord to non-believers. He goes on: "I have given them the glory that you gave me, that they may be one as we are one – I in them and you in me – so that they may be brought to complete unity. Then the world will know that you sent me and have loved them even as you have loved me" (17:22–23).

Jesus is just about to be arrested and yet His focus is on praying for all believers that they will be "one". He obviously considered it very important! Thankfully, it is not dependent on us; God is at work in us by His Holy Spirit. The theologian R. V. G. Tasker puts it helpfully:

> *This unity, like the love which produces it, is supernatural; it is fundamentally the same as the unity that exists between Father and Son... The perfection of this unity will only be reached so long as the believers keep in touch with their exalted Lord and contemplate the glory which has been His from eternity.*[1]

The reason we are highlighting this passage is a deep sense that, as a church in this nation, we are again in a time of struggle to "be one". We do not just struggle in a wider national sense to "be one" but also in our individual congregations. This is not rocket science – we are, after all, still human and we have always found it a challenge to operate as the body of Christ because of our differing opinions, because of our fallen characters and behaviour, and due to our pride.

When we reflect on centuries past we see a church continually unsure about whether it could be "one" as Jesus prayed it would. David King, who looked at local unity in Scotland in approximately 1851, pressed and stressed the need for unity ahead of doctrinal debate and controversy: "Unity, as Christ prayed for it, was to be visible so that the world might believe. Unity was simply a means, with the end being people coming to faith in Christ."[2] He, along with other evangelicals debating around the same time, was seeking to bring evangelical unity. The Evangelical Alliance has sought to implement this unity across denominations and across the ages, beginning in 1845 in Liverpool where leaders agreed that there was "sufficient common ground among disparate Evangelicals to put in place a new body, with a basic doctrinal framework, which was committed to a broadly based unity".[3] It has always been challenging to find enough to agree on and maintain unity over. Each denomination has struggled over the decades and still does today. The Baptist Union maintains the "one body" with their Declaration of Principle;[4] however, ministers still struggle with the tension of so few words, arguing the need for a lengthier statement.

Recent issues have divided opinion and taken us down a track of discussion that can take us off the focus of the Great Commission and ultimately the One who calls us. Jesus never said "don't have opinions", but He did want us to maintain sight of our mission. The enemy would like to distract us from the glory found in being one and make us so broken and divided that every weapon formed against us will prosper!

It is interesting to note that where there is persecution in the world, there is so often church growth. We both have memories from trips to countries such as Ethiopia and Sudan, where we've seen first-hand a church under pressure and struggling with persecution. In these contexts the church has been growing massively. As one Ethiopian pastor said when quoting the second-century early Christian writer Tertullian, "The blood of the martyrs is the seed of the church." We need to know our position and rid ourselves of the mess that so easily entangles us, but let us fix our eyes on Jesus and run the race marked out for us together.

We love the verses in Hebrews 12:1–2:

> *Therefore, since we are surrounded by such a great cloud of witnesses, let us throw off everything that hinders and the sin that so easily entangles. And let us run with perseverance the race marked out for us, fixing our eyes on Jesus, the pioneer and perfecter of faith. For the joy set before him he endured the cross, scorning its shame, and sat down at the right hand of the throne of God.*

We are surrounded by a cloud of witnesses who are part of "one body" with us, encouraging us to be "one as Jesus is one with the Father and the Spirit". Let's not be "one" if and when persecution hits our nation, but let's unite to reflect the glory of God and radiate Him to the lost.

Anne remembers leading a mission team in a small town a little over a decade ago, and beginning the week focusing on the passage in John 17 and praying together that they would maintain unity as a team and see the glory of God. After a week of fun activities drawing many young people together across the area, they had an evening of sharing the gospel and worshipping with them through song. Many of the young people that they encountered that week gave their lives to Christ; it was incredible! When they fed back to the mission team at the end of their time with them, many of the young people said that there was "something different about them" that was attractive. Added to this they said they "loved the way the team loved one another and worked together". Not one bad word was spoken about anyone, to anyone else, that week. The glory of God was at work amongst the team, showing the young people Jesus.

THE MISSIONAL BODY

So many writers are acknowledging the need for our focus to shift to a more "missional" approach. As a church we are coming out of the Christendom era and we cannot rest on our laurels in an ever-changing culture. The body of Christ is just that: "a body" that does not stand still but moves out into the community as "one". The core of it stays the same: the heart beats with the love of Jesus, the lungs breathe out the truth of Christ's death and resurrection, and the soul's foundation is built on the Word of God revealed by the Spirit. The mission stays the same but the way that we make disciples looks different. Alan Hirsch and Michael Frost identify the new shape needed for the missional church: "It will place a high value on communal life, more open leadership structures, and the contribution of all the people of God... It will strive for a type of unity in diversity as it celebrates individual differences and values uniqueness, while also placing a high premium on community."[5]

They go on to quote Bishop Gladwin, who concludes, "So the Church will focus on core faith, on minimum essential order, on people and their gifts, on flexible patterns of life held together in communion and on a shared sense of community."[6] What strikes above all is this word "community" and the need within that to know the part we play and see every part of the body as equal. There is a huge shift in terms of leadership – losing the hierarchical approach and instead releasing everyone to contribute. This does not mean that we lose leadership – we have to have clear voices of direction – but we need leaders who are not afraid to release the members of the body. Without each person exercising what God has called them to, there is a piece of the puzzle missing and the body of Christ suffers and is not as strong as it could be.

The struggle with this lies in the nature of society and the constant busyness that we live in. We cannot count the number of meetings that we have attended where people have said, "but I don't have time". Just trying to organize a week of prayer at church was a nightmare for one of our elders, and he was hugely disappointed at the end when he reflected on "seven members coming a number of times in the week, out of one hundred and fifty possibilities". The challenge of being the body together is affected by social media, family problems, work/life balance, global relationships, and other factors. We have constant distractions that fight to take our eyes off the mission of God, and sadly they often win.

Just recently we heard a preacher asking, "Where is our desperate need for God?" He said that if we had a hunger and desire for Jesus that was greater than anything else, then we would want to give our "everything" to Him. He isn't limited by our personal limitations; He is a God who can, and does, work wonders in us and through us, wherever we find ourselves. He might just want to change our list of priorities and challenge our selfish behaviour to help us to see that we are part of something greater than us.

DON'T GO ALONE

Moses knew from the outset that he couldn't embark on the Lord's mission alone. His questioning shows us his humanity and his need for others to assist him. The Lord responds, "You shall speak to him (Aaron) and put words in his mouth; I will help both of you speak and will teach you what to do. He will speak to the people for you, and it will be as if he were your mouth and as if you were God to him" (Exodus 4:15–16). God uses us in what we can do and then He provides others to share the work. Chatting with some leaders recently, one said, "But I doubt I can do what Jesus is asking me to do and so I have been putting it off." The response to her from the rest of the room was "God will give you other people to do the bits that you cannot: just go for it and trust Him." So often we have an idea of how something looks and we make it all about us and what we can do. The Spirit wants to remind us that we are in it with others and that "God has placed the parts in the body, every one of them, just as he wanted them to be" (1 Corinthians 12:18). As the writer and philosopher Benjamin Franklin said, "Don't put off until tomorrow what you can do today." Go and do it and trust that along the way God will provide exactly what you need when you need it.

The Lord provided Moses with people to fulfil all sorts of different roles at just the right moments. Notably, Jethro came to visit Moses at the perfect time (Exodus 18). He sees Moses handling everything alone and recommends that he "select capable men from all the people – men who fear God, trustworthy men who hate dishonest gain – and appoint them as officials over thousands, hundreds, fifties and tens" (18:21). Jethro sees that the work is too heavy for Moses and helps him to work out a plan to spread the load. God sends him at just the right moment and shows him the value of utilizing the gifts of others. Even if the Lord is speaking to us about something that He wants us to do, **you can guarantee that He will be raising up others to see, speak, and act on our behalf so that we are not alone**.

We have a choice. We can hobble on alone or we can ask God to send help. We can sit on our dreams and prevent the body of Christ from flourishing. We can let fear and low self-worth prevent us from seeing what God is doing and how He wants to use us as part of His plan on earth. We can think that we are standing on our own but the truth is that we are part of a great family of God that we will worship with for all eternity. Jesus reminds us that "in My Father's house there are many rooms; if it were not so, I would have told you. I am going there to prepare a place for you" (John 14:2). We are called to be a united body of believers who He wants to build up together in Him and one day take us to be with Him where He is. At no point does He desire that we feel alone.

This starts with us realizing that we are part of a body, with many who have gone before, and many who are yet to come. We are part of a body that began over two thousand years ago, was empowered by the Holy Spirit, and goes on being equipped and released today. The story is not finished and won't be until Jesus comes again! We are a body, and if one part of the body is not working then we are all the poorer for it. The body is not made up of one part, but of many. It's in our differences that we are more useful too. It's brilliant we are not all the same, as diversity is needed in function, character, and output. Paul puts it this way in 1 Corinthians 12:17–19:

> *If the whole body were an eye, where would the sense of hearing be? If the whole body were an ear, where would the sense of smell be? But in fact God has placed the parts in the body, every one of them,*

*just as he wanted them to be. If they were all one
part, where would the body be?*

We need each other and it's the different roles we play whilst remaining one body that makes the church so formidable!

There are many reasons why we might not work with others, such as suspicion, mistrust or lack of relationship. For some of us it will be the stuff about us that we've accepted as reality when it might not be. The missional entrepreneur Laurence Singlehurst says that many of us live with a "negative script" about ourselves because of what we've faced or been through. Now don't get us wrong: we do need to acknowledge the journey we've been on, but we also need to change the script of ourselves. We are who God made us to be, not the lies we've been told. In other areas too we need to see that though we are different we are also similar and one body. We sometimes need to learn to value each other and find humour in our differences, not conflict, and work together. One such area would be in ethnic diversity. The Evangelical Alliance's One People Commission has seen significant bridges built across previous ethnic boundaries. As the Senior Pastor of Jesus House, in London, and the UK overseer of the Redeemed Christian Church of God (RCCG), Pastor Agu Irukwu said recently to a bunch of white leaders, "We're brothers with the same Father but different mothers!" As it says in Galatians 3:28, "There is neither Jew nor Gentile, neither slave nor free, nor is there male and female, for you are all one in Christ Jesus." We are one body!

In recent months Gavin has been privileged to find himself speaking in many different cultural contexts within the UK church. This has been a real pleasure and a delight to see the Lord on the move powerfully across so many ethnicities. The wonderful thing is that we remain one body in Christ even though we sometimes do things differently. In heaven there will not be separate sections for different ages, races, genders or anything else. We will all be united in worshipping for eternity. We need to do all we can to embrace being part of a dynamic and diverse body of Christ in the UK.

Just as we are stronger together so too we struggle together. Paul goes on to say in 1 Corinthians 12:26–27, "If one part suffers, every part suffers with it; if one part is honoured, every part rejoices with it. Now you are the body of Christ, and each one of you is a part of it." Whatever lies you may have been told, and whatever realities you may live with, you are part of this body and as a body we function together, we rejoice together, and we mourn together. Just like with the football World Record, without everyone bringing to the party that which they are, the whole is weaker. We may seem fragile as individuals but as a body and a collective we are strong!

Maybe you are someone who knows the part that they play but needs to use their gifts in a different way. Perhaps you have buried your talents and need to ask God or a friend to help you to uncover them again. Maybe you are someone God uses prophetically and know that the Spirit is revealing other people's gifts to you, and you need to begin to help them to own them and walk in how God has equipped them. Or perhaps you are someone who needs to hear these words: "We start with you. What are your strengths and how can you capitalize on them? What are your most powerful combinations? Where do they take you? What one, two or three things can you do better than ten thousand other people?"[7] Whatever these gifts are we need them as part of the body, as we are stronger together. We have a cause that's bigger than any one church, ministry or organization: the transformation of our nation for Christ.

YES! But how?

YOU AND GOD

Where do I fit in the body? Consider the questions below:

- What are my strengths of character?
- What can I do well?
- What am I capable of doing in my lifetime?
- What supernatural gifts do I/could I/should I be exercising?
- Where do I fit in terms of the Body of Christ?
- Whom could I serve with?

Why not take these questions to someone you trust and ask them for their answers about you.

Then answer them for your friend.

Pray for these truths to become a reality for one another.

Personality tests

Myers Briggs is a personality assessment that evaluates how people see the world and make decisions. It helps you understand yourself better. E.g. are you an extrovert or an introvert? Find the test here:

www.myersbriggs.org/my-mbti-personality-type/take-the-mbti-instrument/

Strengths Finder is a great tool to identify you and/or your team's strengths and put them to the best use. It helps every individual understand and utilise their 5 key strengths:

www.gallupstrengthscenter.com/home

What is your SHAPE?

Take a moment to consider your "SHAPE" (Spiritual Gifts, Heart, Abilities, Personality, Experience). There's an online test for this available here:

https://www.cpas.org.uk/advice-and-support/exploring-call/your-shape/build-your-shape

List what you think your three key things are under each heading. Are you currently making use of them all? Consider how any neglected features could be used.

GROUP ACTIVITY

1. Read John 17 together – Jesus' final prayers before He is arrested. His biggest focus is on unity for believers, so that unbelievers will see His glory and be drawn to Christ. Ask the group: are they living in unity with others? Are there any people in their lives with whom they are struggling? Could God be asking them to forgive and be reconciled?

Pray for those who are finding relationships hard and need the Lord's strength to put things right and live differently. Ask Jesus to unite the group so that His glory can be seen and more lives drawn to Him.

2. Think about the global church. It is part of the body of Christ. Take a look at 1 Corinthians 12:26–27: "If one part suffers, every part suffers with it." Which parts of the global church are struggling and suffering? How is it affecting us? What are we doing/can we do about it? Share ideas and thoughts. Why not stand together and pray for the church around the world; pray for Christians who are being persecuted. Pray that together we can stand for Christ no matter what comes against us. You may want to link arms as a display of unity.

Further reading

M. Buckingham, *Now Discover Your Strengths* (London: Pocket Books, 2004)
B. Bugbee, *What You Do Best in the Body of Christ* (Grand Rapids: Zondervan, 2005)

9
Playing Our Part

"Lord, when I feel that what I'm doing is insignificant and unimportant, help me to remember that everything I do is significant and important in your eyes, because you love me and you put me here, and no one else can do what I am doing in exactly the way I do it."

BRENNAN MANNING

We often think that **the church is in many ways the most under-appreciated pillar of our UK society**. The church makes a huge contribution to all levels of society, yet it often feels that the only press we get is negative. There seems a reluctance in the media to champion the church as a force for good, perhaps due in part to a desire to be "politically correct". Behind closed doors many are happy to acknowledge the incredible impact that is made by the church, but in public this is not always the case. The scores of mums and toddler groups, Friday night youth clubs, and support in community hubs like schools is just the tip of the iceberg for the church's contribution to society. In recent years this has all accelerated somewhat too, as Christians have stepped in to fill many of the gaps in a society deeply impacted by global economic uncertainty. Into this unstable landscape the church has been behind many new initiatives that are having huge impacts, such as Street Pastors, Foodbanks, and CAP Centres (to mention but three).

Yet for all our contributions we still can't help but think there must be more! If the church fully got going with a desire to change this land, the mind boggles at quite what might be possible. We could truly see complete change in this island. This nation could be turned around and we could see something we've only read or daydreamed about before. If the whole church took on the mandate to reach our land then nothing would be impossible. We could see our streets and communities transformed and our nation living for Christ. The game in Britain really could be changed!

Jesus said, "I am the way and the truth and the life. No one comes to the Father except through me" (John 14:6). Therefore He is not an option; He's the meaning behind the universe, the mediator between the Father and His children, the One who died in our place that we might live. As the founding and Senior Pastor of Willow Creek Community Church in Illinois, USA, Bill Hybels, famously said, **"There is nothing like the church when it's working right. The local church is the hope of the world."** When we carry the message of Christ we can change the world. We carry this truth and must speak up when prompted or needed, just as Moses did.

We can never be just a social arm of society. Yes, we Christians must have a heart for social justice and we must care for the least. Jesus modelled a great heart for the poor and for social transformation and we too share this DNA. Nonetheless, we are not called to deliver some strange form of sanctified humanism that is all action and entirely lacking in words, and that benefits society but doesn't see people accepting Jesus as their personal Lord and Saviour. We the church are called to bring about cultural revolution in this land for Christ, on every level. We are not called primarily to serve the government's plans but instead to serve the agenda of Christ. If the two are achieved at the same time, then great, but we know the one we must be targeting first! It's all too easy to follow the agenda of those offering statutory funding, but we must not allow such things to then dictate what we can or can't do within society. We are here to transform our society, not just to become a passive part within it. We are an active people needing to get our hands dirty for Christ.

WITH WHAT IDEOLOGY?

The church is on a mission to the world. So often it can feel like we have no chance of success, and yet God is bigger than all the rubbish around us. We need to keep reminding ourselves that we need to see things with the right perspective. This world says, "Tell your God how big your problems are. The Lord says tell your problems how big your God is."[1] God is bigger than anything, and we need to play our part in bringing His abundant hope to a nation in need. He is bigger than the doubters, the antagonists, the sceptics, the intellectuals; the list is endless. We need to grow confidence in this great big God!

For our mission to be effective it must involve both lifestyle and proclamation. Word and deed must go together. Jesus may have told us, "whatever you did for one of the least of these brothers and sisters of mine, you did for me" (Matthew 25:40), but he also specifically instructed that we should "Go into all the world and preach the gospel to all creation" (Mark 16:15). Deeds and words give a context to one another, but one alone can never be good enough. It is often argued that the church does more youth work than the state. However, without sharing the gospel as a part of this youth work, how are our efforts any different to those that the state would provide? Depriving young people of the spiritual dimension of life does not invalidate initiatives aimed at their physical and emotional well-being, but it does remove the one lifeline that would truly transform their life for now and their destiny for eternity.

St Francis of Assisi has been widely quoted as saying, "Preach the gospel at all times. If necessary, use words." It seems that we have gone to the extreme of attempting to preach the gospel while believing that we needn't use words. We have often become terrified to declare the name of Jesus, because of what we fear people's response might be. The dynamic preacher Jeff Lucas referred to this situation in his monthly column for *Premier Christianity* magazine: "Some of us have packed up using words altogether. But the chap who said that was none other than St. Francis of Assisi, famous not only for chatting with squirrels, but also for giving away everything that he owned. When you've donated all you have to the poor because of your love for Jesus, you probably don't have to use that many words."[2]

Like fashions these things seem to go in cycles. A generation or so ago the church in Britain used lots of words and needed to capture a stronger social heart. However, here we are a little later on and it feels like we have a strong social heart and need to discover words again, without losing the social gospel at the same time. We don't need a pendulum shift back to words but to keep the social engagement as strongly as we have it and to add words to that to bring balance. Besides, how could you preach the gospel without words? Surely that's like having a BBQ without meat!

We know the power of the name of Jesus and are only too aware that it provokes a multitude of responses, both positive and negative. A passage in 1 Corinthians sums it up well: "For the message of the cross is foolishness to those who are perishing, but to us who are being saved it is the power of God" (1:18). However, we as Christians must never let the apparent offensiveness of the gospel prevent us from accepting and using the power behind it. We have seen far too many missions in which all we actually do is entertain people, without telling them who it is that we live for. By so doing we can deny them that truth which alone will provide the answer to the search of their lives.

Our postmodern Western church can often appear to have become ashamed of the gospel. This is in such clear contrast to Paul, who says in Romans 1:14–16: "I am obligated both to Greeks and non-Greeks, both to the wise and the foolish. That is why I am so eager to preach the gospel also to you who are in Rome. For I am not ashamed of the gospel, because it is the power of God that brings salvation to everyone who believes." Paul would not need telling twice that he was required to share his faith in every context in which he found himself. Many might say, "but it was different for him" and "he had it easier". This is simply not the case. By this stage Paul had been engaged in his ministry for almost thirty exhausting years. During this time he had experienced all manner of disheartening things. This apostle had lived through enough trauma, excitement, and difficulty to last most people ten lifetimes. He would have had the most compellingly legitimate reasons and arguments for giving up on sharing his faith; yet, in contrast to what you might expect, his enthusiasm did not run out. He knew that **if good people stay silent, then bad things happen!**

Paul's three bold statements – "I am obligated", "I am eager", and "I am not ashamed" – clearly contradict the attitude of many Christians today. John Stott points out that too often we appear to regard evangelism as an optional extra, and feel in some perverse sense that if we do engage in it then we are doing God some sort of favour! It's as if He owes us something for bothering to share! The postmodern mood is often one of reluctance and fear; Paul's was one of eagerness and enthusiasm.[3] We need to seek to regain some of this necessary eagerness. When Christ tells us to change and become like children (Matthew 18:3), we don't for a moment think this means anything immature. What we believe He means, in part, is to recapture the eagerness and enthusiasm of those days as children. We have two young children, and whatever the previous day may have carried, by the next morning they are enthusiastic and eager, ready for a new day and the fresh start that it brings. They get excited about everything, smile a lot, and so often see the best where we might see the worst. This is the kind of childlike attitude we need to adopt in reaching the world too.

In our postmodern world many would also argue that it was a very different cultural context that Paul operated within and therefore the rules of engagement were entirely different. How could he possibly manage to do the same in our instant and consumerist world? Surely that was beyond even Paul. However, the world Paul found himself in was no easy place to minister either. He was in a very difficult cultural context where sharing the gospel was at least as untenable and unpopular as it might ever seem here. Rome was perceived in her day as the ultimate symbol of imperial power and pride. People spoke of it in awe, and many hoped to visit it on some kind of pilgrimage at least once in their lifetime in order simply to look and stare in wonder at her beauty. The city was seen as the pinnacle of human creation and as evidence that human strength was all that was needed. This context of Rome would have been so hostile to the message Paul carried of a greater power, of a humble, yet almighty, King.

As if this wasn't bad enough, according to tradition Paul was no "pin up" of a man. He is said to have been small, with eyebrows that met in the middle, skinny rickety legs, a bald patch, bent nose, poor eyesight, and no great rhetorical gifts. What could this one man, Paul, hope to accomplish when pitched against the proud might of imperial Rome? Would it not be more sensible to stay away? Or, if he must visit Rome, should he not keep quiet, to avoid being laughed out of town?[4] Paul did not think so. He was brave and stood up to the popular culture. If a man of this appearance in such a city of pride and power believed he could truly change things and share the gospel, then what on earth is stopping us? None of us claims to be anything but imperfect, but we do follow a perfect God who's with us in it all; as such, we can be braver, clearer, and bolder. Spiritual hindsight is once more an amazing reality, as, looking on two thousand years later, Paul was right. The great ancient city of Rome is in ruins and Jesus is alive!

WHAT ABOUT NOW?

Whether we like it or not, a number of us may actually, at times, be ashamed of the gospel. We may deny this outright as being even a faint possibility, but Jesus clearly identified it as a danger when He warned his disciples in Luke 9:26, "Whoever is ashamed of me and my words, the Son of Man will be ashamed of them when he comes in his glory and in the glory of the Father and of the holy angels." It is not so long after this that Peter, the alleged rock, is ashamed of Jesus and denies Him in Luke 22:54–62. We must fight against fear and be prepared to witness with boldness to a needy world. For if those who have come to know the truth are not prepared to proclaim it, then how can we complain when others do not know the truth? It has wisely been observed, **"It is better to light a candle than to grumble about the darkness."**

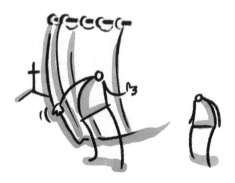

Recently Gavin spoke at a men's conference, and although he'd been told the room was full of Christians he still did a gospel call at the end of his talk. Seven men made a decision to follow Jesus and it was his delight to pray with them. At lunchtime the organizer of the conference came to find Gavin. He was absolutely buzzing after seeing the men make a decision for Christ. He said with real enthusiasm that he was blown away by it, and that they hadn't seen a single decision the year before at the same event. Gavin asked him simply, "Did you ask people if they wanted to follow Jesus last year?" The answer was "no". **We can't expect people to come to faith by osmosis**; sometimes we need to make the invitation. We need to pray for the self-assurance to step out, knowing that whatever the outcome the Lord is with us. We wonder if at times we are simply not seeing as much fruit as we would like because we are not asking the question enough.

Some of us are not ashamed. In contrast, what is stopping many of us from sharing our faith is the fact that we just cannot accept any inherent value or intrinsic good in either ourselves or our actions. Low self-esteem poses a massive problem in our society and therefore in the contemporary church. Whenever someone struggles with thinking that they have nothing to offer, our minds always turn immediately to the feeding of the five thousand as recorded in John 6. When you include women and children as well, you discover that there were somewhere between eleven and fifteen thousand hungry people in a field at lunchtime. Jesus asks where they should buy bread (verse 5), and no one knows what to do until Andrew finds a boy's packed lunch. He bravely takes it up to Jesus and says, "Here is a boy with five small barley loaves and two small fish, but how far will they go among so many?" (verse 9).

Andrew cannot understand how this small offering will help, but despite his lack of spiritual awareness he still knows enough to bring it to Jesus. He acknowledges that the packed lunch before him is not even adequate to feed one hungry man, but he is working with a Jesus who works wonders and so he takes it to the King. As a result, Jesus feeds the whole field with plenty to spare. Andrew is probably as surprised as the rest, but he is beginning to realize that this Jesus can take what seem like small efforts to us and use them in incredible ways. He can take the little that we have to offer and do things with inadequate resources that we would never dream to be possible. The plain and simple reality is that with Jesus on our side anything can happen.

For this reason, when we think we have nothing to offer, we must still bring it to Jesus. If we consider that He could use it incredibly, then we may well see this belief fulfilled! It is fundamental that as a church we must start witnessing and living out our faith in every environment that we find ourselves in. We must bring our little and watch Jesus use it amazingly. Just as He took a boy's packed lunch and fed thousands of people, He can take our small efforts and use them in incredible ways.

It is of paramount importance that we avoid beating ourselves up by unfair comparisons. Some people tell amazing stories of leading people to Jesus on trains, in parks, and all over the place. Such tales can make the rest of us feel like we can never live up to these standards. Let us be clear on something – we can't! We are living testimonies of God's grace, not people collecting Hollywood stories. We met a girl recently who was feeling really discouraged. She desperately wanted her four college friends to come to faith, and none of them were. However, as we probed with questions it became clear that these four had all been really hostile to Christ a year or so earlier and now, as a result of this girl, they were no longer hostile though equally not yet all that interested. We turned to the girl and said, "You should be delighted, as your friends are on a journey and you are positively influencing them for Christ, even if the progress may seem slow." We need to celebrate the impact we are making in the everyday, not just the "Kairos" moments.

WHAT NEXT?

Every element of our lives needs to be committed to making Jesus known. In his book, *The Life*, J. John writes:

> **We live in hard times for heroes**. *There is a cynicism in our culture that eats away at even the most glorious reputations. Almost overnight, selfless geniuses turn out to be selfish fools, great leaders are revealed as insecure bullies and champions of morality are exposed as hypocrites. One of the few figures to survive with their reputation intact is Jesus Christ.*[5]

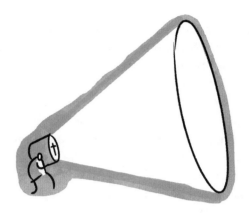

We need to work as a church so that the same can be said in the West in a hundred or a thousand years' time. We must not let the name or reputation of Jesus become diminished. We need to do this in every sphere and area of our lives too. When we started studying at the London School of Theology (then London Bible College) in 1998, we were both greatly challenged and inspired by the then vice-principal, Mark Greene. He was a massively dynamic and powerful communicator. It was he who taught us both the basics of communication for the first time.

At the end of our first year Mark left and has gone on to make a huge impact in the area of workplace ministry. This is the idea of making a difference for Christ where you are and in the place you spend most of your time – work. In his recent book *Fruitfulness on the Frontline*, Mark talks about six "Ms" that provide a framework for fruitfulness. These are: 1) modelling godly character, 2) making good work, 3) ministering grace and love, 4) moulding culture, 5) being a mouthpiece for truth and justice, and 6) being a messenger of the gospel.[6] These six things lived out properly make a huge difference not just to the workplace but the family, sports team, social club, etc. All of us can do each of these six things and bring about change in the environments we find ourselves in – on our frontlines. We cannot rely on the gathered church to change the nation; it's when we are all released into our everyday environments that real differences can take place.

We must fight to establish our Lord's relevance and **stop an increasingly secularized world from forgetting who Jesus is**. We can all do this. We can all be salt and light in our own environments. We all have colleagues, neighbours, and friends that the church may struggle to impact through any other means than us. So let's get active. As two famous lines from the *Chronicles of Narnia* say, **"Aslan is on the move" and "He's not a tame lion."** God is doing great things and we need to play our part and join in with Him. He is active and desires to use us to fulfil His purposes in our environments. Greene puts it this way: "God is at work. And God has been at work in his people, in his church, in this land. And, no doubt, in you, in a myriad ways. We may not get to see the outcome in our lifetimes, but it is so. And so, the Lord be with you, whatever hat you wear. The Lord be with you on your frontline."[7]

It is certainly not all about the church and its buildings. We need to be involved in society on every level and in each environment. It's about us as Christians taking responsibility, knowing that we speak and act under the authority of God. It means caring about the place where God has put us, and stepping up, speaking out, and engaging in public life. It's about taking our place in politics, the media, and all parts of society,[8] bringing about change in His name!

As the bride of Christ let's take up this call to be mobilized into action, to realize our ambition of touching a small part of our world for Jesus on our own unique frontlines. We must believe that our part is worthwhile, and wherever we find ourselves – from the classroom, to the workplace, to the

family dinner table, to the nightclub or the football pitch –
we need to share something of the story of Jesus. Every one
of us has a unique part to play in reaching the world with this
incredible good news. Let us each make sure that we play it!

YES! But how?

YOU AND GOD

Not everyone is a born evangelist, but we can all be witnesses for Jesus. Make a list of all the people you encounter in a normal week. For each person, think about how Jesus would be "good news" for them. Pray for them. Decide on how you might bring Jesus into the conversation next time you meet.

Consider...

- How do you feel about talking about Jesus?
- When was the last time that you mentioned the name of Jesus in the company of people who don't believe?
- Does it make you feel afraid?
- Are you more inclined to deed than to word?
- How might we bring Jesus more into the centre of all we do?
- How can we live more distinctively?

Tools to focus on Christ:

Alexander Hamilton, founding father of the United States, said this:

> ## "THOSE WHO STAND FOR NOTHING FALL FOR ANYTHING."
> ### – ALEXANDER HAMILTON

Consider: what do you stand for?

Remembering who He is and what He has done, should we be standing for Him more?

Listen:

"This I Believe (The Creed)" by Hillsong Worship, from the album *This I Believe* (you may be able to access the song and lyrics online).

GROUP ACTIVITY

1. **Read Romans 1:14–16**

   The apostle Paul: "I am *obligated* both to Greeks and non-Greeks, both to the wise and the foolish. That is why I am so *eager* to preach the gospel also to you who are in Rome. For I am *not ashamed* of the gospel, because it is the power of God that brings salvation to everyone who believes: first to the Jew, then to the Gentile." Ask the group, do they feel like Paul? Hands up? How many struggle with sharing the gospel, hands up? Do they feel eager but ashamed?

   Why not agree together to try to get Jesus into conversation with a non-believer in the week ahead and then report back to each other on how it went. Pray for the group that they would have God's power to share Jesus.

2. Mark Greene talks about six "Ms" that provide a framework for fruitfulness. These are: 1) modelling godly character, 2) making good work, 3) ministering grace and love, 4) moulding culture, 5) being a mouthpiece for truth and justice, and 6) being a messenger of the gospel. Chat together about each one, asking each other if you are

doing them and how you might share Christ more. Pray for the Holy Spirit to strengthen and equip the church in these areas.

USEFUL WEBSITES

Help, advice & resources to live out your faith in public contexts:

www.thepublicleader.com

A resource helping people understand where, and how, they can share their faith in public settings:

www.eauk.org/speakup

Further reading

K. Costa, *God at Work: Living Every Day with Purpose* (London: Alpha International, 2013)

M. Greene, *Fruitfulness on the Frontline* (Nottingham: Inter-Varsity Press, 2014)

M. Greene, *Thank God it's Monday* (Milton Keynes: Scripture Union, 2001)

Part 4

EQUIP

Numbers 13:25 – 14:9

10
The Voice of the Few

"If you hear a voice within you say 'you cannot paint,' then by all means paint, and that voice will be silenced."

VINCENT VAN GOGH

When we were younger we were both big *Star Wars* fans, though over the years our enthusiasm for it has waned considerably. However, having kids has seen the world of Yoda, R2-D2, and friends re-enter our lives with a vengeance. Like many, we love the original films but view the more recent prequels with a little disdain. There is one storyline, however, that is particularly intriguing to us in the prequels: that of the reality of who Anakin Skywalker chooses to listen to on his road to becoming one of the greatest Hollywood baddies of all time, Darth Vader. Anakin is trained in the skills of Jedi by perennial good guy Obi-Wan Kenobi. Obi-Wan is always there for him and on hand with great input and advice, but Anakin, more often than not, chooses to ignore this. Anakin always shows greater potential than those around him, and his lust for instant power, success, and respect quickly get him into trouble.

Around him is another influence, Senator Palpatine, who is clearly not a good guy. He promises Anakin all that he wants and quickly. He guarantees him power beyond anything he could have imagined. He waves in front of Anakin all that he could ever want; all Anakin has to do is compromise his integrity and turn from good to bad and he will get it. The scenes are somewhat reminiscent of the temptations of Jesus by the devil in the wilderness (see Mark 4:1–11). Unlike Christ, Anakin listens to the wrong voice and eventually turns into Darth Vader. Whom we listen to plays such a massive part in what we later become.

Numbers 13–14 echo a similar conversation: what voice are we being led to follow? Is it the one that makes us feel safe or strokes our ego? How do we sift through the voices that we hear, so that we can find the right voice in the crowd? How do we know what the Lord is saying to us over the voices of the many? So often we can think that if the majority of people are saying the same thing to us, then that is obviously the right thing to do or the way to go. Yet here in Numbers we see a clear tiny minority speaking truth that needs picking out, believing in, and standing on. The other challenge is that the Israelites are influencing each other, listening to one another's groans and complaints and then taking them on as their own. The voice of the many gets louder and louder, drowning out the words of the few.

Having been liberated from Egypt and seen the Lord forgive and provide for them in such incredible ways, the Israelites are still trusting in their own opinions and trying to go a different way than God wants them to go. You would have thought that they would have learned their lesson by now! Even as they get to Kadesh and find themselves on the border of the Promised Land – "a land flowing with milk and honey" – they are still disobeying God. As the theologian Gordon Wenham writes, "These chapters should relate how the drama of the Exodus and wilderness wanderings reached a triumphant conclusion."[1] And yet we see a very different outcome – not one of new hope but one of death.

We can be so bad at learning from our previous experiences. God has been so faithful to the Israelites when they've listened to His prompting, and yet here they go with the masses over what's right. We can be like impetuous children, never really learning from our mistakes and doing the same things again, putting our hands into a metaphorical fire time and time again even though we know that last time we did we got burnt. We really can be like sheep getting ourselves into trouble.

THE STORY

We find this narrative in Numbers so helpful for considering whom we are listening to: Moses obeys God (13:1) and sends out twelve spies/leaders of the tribes to explore Canaan, asking for a full report on the land and the people that they find there (3:16–20). After forty days they bring back lush fruit and it is clear that the land is good. This is the land that the Lord their God has promised to lead them into. However, the spies give an interesting report to Moses and Aaron and the whole assembly (13:27–33). It is intriguing to note their first words: **"We went into the land to which you sent us" (verse 27), not "the land that the Lord has promised us"**. They are not taking hold of the Lord's promises, or ownership for this place as somewhere they are meant to live. They do add that the land is flowing with milk and honey but are clearly terrified of the people that live there (13:28–29). The spies spread terrible rumours about the land amongst the Israelites, causing them to cry out in grief and long for a return to Egypt (14:1–4).

However Caleb, one of the spies, cannot agree with the rest of them. He is certain that they "should go up and take possession of the land, for we can certainly do it" (13:30). Caleb and Joshua, who had also explored the land and given positive testimony regarding it (14:7–8), are in the minority. They find themselves in a ten-against-two position, with all the Israelites crying out in distress. Moses and Aaron stay face down before the Lord because they know He will be angry again with the Israelites' grumbling and disobedience.

What is interesting here is that the words of truth and the right way forward are being spoken by the minority. We hear only Caleb and Joshua speak positively about the Promised Land, and believe and stand on the promise that the Lord can bring them into it (14:7–9). The other spies and the rest of the Israelite community that we can hear have allowed fear to confuse their thinking and distort their minds and hearts. Even after seeing miracle after miracle in the desert, they are still unable to trust God to lead them into Canaan.

The Lord has promised to lead his people into a "land flowing with milk and honey", and here is the land. Yet somehow the promise has got buried beneath a load of exaggerated gossip from the spies, so that they have forgotten the clear words from God. So often we can forget what God has said to us before because we are either afraid, in distress, listening to the wrong people or struggling to see further than ourselves. The spies spread a bad report about the land, saying "the land we explored devours those living in it. All the people living there are of great size. We saw the Nephilim living there (the descendants of Anak come from the Nephilim). We seemed like grasshoppers in our own eyes, and we looked the same to them" (13:32–33). The idea of Nephilim scares the people, because it conjures up "demi-gods who lived on earth before the flood" (see Genesis 6:4).[2] These words from the spies distort the reality that lies in front of them. The words cloud the Israelites' vision so that they cannot see and hear the truth from Joshua and Caleb. These words spread fear like wildfire around the assembly so that they can no longer see the way to go.

It reminds us of those verses in Galatians: "You were running a good race. Who cut in on you and kept you from obeying the truth? That kind of persuasion does not come from the one who calls you. 'A little yeast works through the whole batch of dough'" (5:7–9). Words pass from one person to another, affecting and distorting the whole community and stopping us from walking in truth. We love the way Charles Spurgeon describes it: **"A lie can travel half way around the world while the truth is putting on its shoes."**

It is so challenging to hear the voice of the Lord over the crowd. We know that it comes through Caleb and Joshua, because they are echoing the words of God and the truth that He has told them about where He is leading them, but we also see it with hindsight, don't we? As for the men who went to explore the land, only Joshua, son of Nun, and Caleb, son of Jepunneh, survived (Numbers 14:38). Oh Lord, that we would see what is from you and hear the words that come from you. Help us to step back from our situation and see a bigger picture.

Sadly, the Israelite cries to appoint another leader and return to Egypt (14:4) signal their end. Yes, the Lord forgives them (14:20), but they have tested Him so much that the spies will die with a plague (14:37), and the Israelites in the desert (14:35) or the hill country (14:44–45). Their disobedience, to the point of ignoring Moses and pressing on towards the Promised Land, without the ark of the covenant, ends with death. As Wenham writes, "Israel does not take God seriously, or listen to Moses his appointed representative. They will not enter Canaan until they learn their lesson, and that may take a long time."[3]

Two men are giving the right report. Ten are distorting the truth.

WRONG DIRECTION

There is danger in the desert place – danger of temptation, danger of misunderstanding, and danger of going down the wrong path. We remember finding ourselves in the desert about ten years ago. We were questioning "What next?" We felt confused about jobs, about location, about church, and it felt like everything was up for grabs. We began to look for answers. In the midst of boredom, frustration, and cloudiness, we tried to find a way ahead, putting the house on the market, travelling to a new church in a different area, and questioning new job prospects. For ten months we pushed hard at a door and longed for it to open. It didn't. Nothing changed. It wasn't until we got on our knees and surrendered that we realized we were wrong. We had been listening to voices of reason and over-indulging our boredom, in order to change our situation, when God was clearly saying, as He did through Samuel, "Now then, stand still and see this great thing the Lord is about to do before your eyes!" (1 Samuel 12:16). As we stood still, took the house off the market, stopped striving for change, and started listening to Jesus, life began to shift and change at a time and in a way that only God could ordain. It didn't look how we imagined it would and yet it was perfect for us for that season.

We mustn't try to live life thinking that we know the best way; we don't. The Israelites would lose their lives on a quest for what felt right to them, but when we go God's way new worlds open up ahead of us. We see a theme in Scripture of needing to listen carefully for God's voice above the rest. It seems obvious to us that the loudest noise will be the Lord, and yet He never works in a straightforward way – we always have to trust Him. Elijah looks for God in a powerful wind that shatters the rocks and tears the mountains apart; he looks for Him in an earthquake and a fire, but the Lord speaks to him in a gentle whisper (1 Kings 19:11–13). God is not always in the business of shouting the loudest, but teaching us to trust in Him. He doesn't want us to jump to earthly conclusions but to seek His face. Jesus reminds us to "Enter through the narrow gate. For wide is the gate and broad is the road that leads to destruction, and many enter through it. But small is the gate and narrow is the road that leads to life, and only a few find it" (Matthew 7:13–14).

RIGHT WORDS

Hearing the voice of the few and going with them, or even hearing the voice of the Lord and knowing it will not be welcomed, is an extremely challenging place to find ourselves. Many of us can experience this kind of challenge just because we are Christians! We know when we are asked where we are going at Easter it is so much easier to say "Butlins" than to say "a Christian camp called Spring Harvest, at Butlins" – not just because it is a longer sentence, but because we are scared of the reaction that we might get. We have a good friend at church who often hears, feels, and sees things in the Spirit. Other members of the congregation think that it is brilliant, but she says it is very costly. She is in the minority. The words she has for people are hard to hear, but they can bring life and hope to people. If individuals hear the Lord speaking through her and don't dismiss it to go with the majority, they can walk into greater freedom and fruitfulness.

The Christian leader John Wimber recalls a time on an aeroplane when he turned to look at a passenger across the aisle and saw with spiritual eyes the word "adultery" across his forehead. Then the name of a woman dropped into John's mind – he leant across and asked the man, into his ear, if the name meant anything to him. The guy turned pale and they moved up the plane to have a conversation. John felt God tell him to say to the man that "he was committing adultery and that God would take him if he did not repent". After conversation and prayer the man repented and surrendered his life to Christ. He then went and told his wife the whole story and then led her to Christ.[4] What a plane journey! When we read this recently it shook us, not because we don't believe in miracles, but because we sometimes think that we are in danger of not speaking spiritual truths, worrying that they could offend and cause upset. We do need to be certain that what we are sharing is from the Lord. However, in a world of being accepting, inclusive, and politically correct, sin has become a dirty word – let alone something that we would point out to someone! And yet in this instance, John Wimber heard the Lord, spoke up, and saw two lives saved by Jesus. Incredible.

We do not know what people will say or do, but we have to speak up if Jesus is revealing truth to us. Yes, the consequences can be shocking, but we cannot compromise the gospel. Billy Graham, the great evangelist, said, "Our society strives to avoid any possibility of offending anyone – except God!" We cannot let that be true. Yes, when Joshua has finished speaking in Numbers the "whole assembly talked about stoning them" (14:10). Yes, when Stephen stands up and proclaims the truth about Jesus in Acts they "covered their ears and, yelling at the top of their voices, they all rushed at him, dragged him out of the city and began to stone him" (Acts 7:57–58). Yes, standing up for Christ and speaking the truth is something that we can be "stoned" for, and living lives that uphold Spirit and truth might mean we are not welcome as part of the crowd. But Jesus is with us and we can trust His voice more than any other. Our prayer needs to be, "Lord, please fill us with your Holy Spirit; give us ears to hear you, lips that will speak out your truth, and confidence to walk into the life that you have called us to."

Moses, Aaron, Caleb, and Joshua show us that walking God's way is always the best way. It leads to life and hope. The Israelites, along with the ten spies, show us that lack of trust and fear keep us stuck in a state of existing rather than really living. Yes, there were things to conquer in the Promised Land – Caleb and Joshua were not oblivious to that – but no way on earth were they wanting to return to Egypt.

ON GOD'S TERMS NOT MINE

As we first got to know each other within the confines of London School of Theology, Gavin began to share some of his testimony, a key moment being when his parents had moved overseas to America when he was seventeen years old. On the one hand this seemed like a crazy thing, but as I listened to him I could see that some of their decisions had pointed him to Jesus. One of the clearest things I witnessed was the pain, and yet gain, of leaving his family home behind. It was obviously painful to leave the house he had grown up in, and to move in with friends from church, but over the years I have also seen a benefit. Gavin will go anywhere without too much notice, and into anything, for the kingdom of God. What his parents have modelled to him has released him to serve God wholeheartedly without clinging on to human gain.

Interestingly, in the first year of Bible College, Anne's parents sold her childhood home in a very comfortable part of the UK, and moved too – not to America but to North Wales, to run a hotel. Suddenly there was nowhere to stay in the place that she had spent so much of her life so far, and her "roots" were also lifted. It is only in recent years that we can see the benefit of this. At the time it was very painful. As much as Anne knew God was calling her parents to a new location, leaving everything behind was huge. Both families' relocations have released us massively. It took us a while to stop looking back at the past, but we find it fascinating how God has enabled us to look ahead for the Promised Land, instead of remaining in the safety and familiarity of "home".

We can often find ourselves looking back and believing that what we had before was better than what there ever could be again. This state limits our freedom to live fully in the here and now and in what is to come. Nobel Prize-winning author Andre Gide wrote, **"One does not discover new lands without consenting to lose sight of the shore."**[5] If some part of us always longs for what we used to have, we limit what God might have for us tomorrow. Yes, there will be challenges ahead of us, but they will make us more dependent on Jesus and take us into a deeper relationship with Him.

We hear so many people speak of their "house for life" or their "decision to settle for good" and it is challenging. Culture says that what is familiar and safe, where family dwell and friends are found, is the best and only place for us to be. And yet the Lord lived a life saying, "Foxes have dens and birds have nests, but the Son of Man has no place to lay his head" (Matthew 8:20). We know people that declare that God would have to "shout it from the rooftops" to get them to move, and we think to ourselves, "Why would He bother?!" Don't hear us wrong; we know many people whom God has called to commit to areas and people groups for the long haul, but we think it is when the mentality becomes "all about me and what we want as a family", not about what God wants for us, that we have a problem.

The Lord did not want the Israelites to return to Egypt. He had rescued them from slavery. Their memories of it were so tainted from reality! Their ability to trust God for an incredible new home and future, along with their ability to lean on Him every day, was so limited, even though they saw the miracles before them. God is greater than everything we see. In a world of uncertainty we need to cling to Him, rather than to our human understanding. We love the words that Malcolm Duncan writes when he says, "The Kingship of Jesus meant that Herod could not be King. It means that the Greek philosophers could not be king. It means that reason could not be king. Nothing else can be king when Jesus is King."[6] The cross stands above it all, and we can trust Jesus with our whole lives, with everything we were, are, and will ever be.

The bit of the passage that cuts us to the core is at the end of chapter 14 in Numbers, where Moses says to the Israelites, "Do not go up, because the Lord is not with you" (14:42). By this point they have stopped listening to Moses altogether and have fully decided that they know the best way. Ultimately their fear, lack of faith, and their grumbling stop them from entering the Promised Land. How easy it is to completely miss what the Lord is saying to us!

YES! But how?

YOU AND GOD

Consider...

- Whose voice do you listen to the most?
- Are you someone who follows the crowd or decides for yourself?
- Is there a situation that you are faced with at the moment, where you need to hear the voice of God?
- Maybe He is speaking in the voice of the few...?
- Is there any situation where God is asking you to be the voice of truth?
- Do you need to swim in a different direction to the crowd in order to serve Jesus?
- Is it time to start being more of an influencer of others than one who is influenced by the crowd?
- Are you listening to God's voice or the lies of the enemy?
- Perhaps you want to reflect on the words below and remind yourself and those around you what Jesus says to you, stamping Satan's tactics under your foot!

GOD'S VOICE	SATAN'S VOICE
- stills you	- rushes you
- leads you	- pushes you
- reassures you	- frightens you
- enlightens you	- confuses you
- encourages you	- discourages you
- comforts you	- worries you
- calms you	- obsesses you

Who are you following? Is it Jesus? His voice leads the way to a hope and a future.

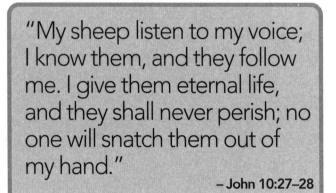

"My sheep listen to my voice; I know them, and they follow me. I give them eternal life, and they shall never perish; no one will snatch them out of my hand."

– John 10:27–28

GROUP ACTIVITY

1. Perhaps as a group you could look at the table above: God's voice and Satan's voice. Ask them to consider what voice they are listening to at the moment? In what areas has Satan's voice been winning in their lives? Perhaps they feel afraid or condemned or confused. In pairs pray for one another, saying sorry for believing the lies of the enemy and asking Jesus to speak His truth to you. Pray John 10:27 over them, asking God to protect their minds and give them the strength to follow Him. Declare 1 John 4:18 over them: "There is no fear in love. But perfect love drives out fear, because fear has to do with punishment..." Ask the Holy Spirit to reveal more of the Father's love to His children.

2. Read Numbers 13–14 together or give a summary of the chapters, picking out particular key notes; for example, we only hear Caleb and Joshua speak positively about

the Promised Land, believing and standing on the promise that the Lord can bring them into it (14:7–9). Ask those assembled if they struggle to go against the flow. Raise a hand if they do. Point out that even in this moment, there is a moment of challenge to be honest and raise a hand, and yet this is in a room full of Christians! Caleb and Joshua stayed focused on what God had said to them. What has God promised you? He will do it. Pray for courage to stand up for God and to go against the crowd. Share testimonies to encourage one another of when you have listened to God and been faithful to what He has asked.

Further reading

J. Huggett, *Listening to God: Hearing His Voice* (London: Hodder & Stoughton, 2010)
A. W. Tozer, *The Pursuit of God* (Chicago: Tate Publishing, 2013)

11
Who Are You Listening to?

"There's a lot of difference between listening and hearing."

G. K. CHESTERTON

rowing up, the loudest voice that Anne could hear was her mother's. It was the voice that told her what she needed to do: "Get dressed, Anne"; "Get your coat on, we are going out", "Do up those shoelaces"; and "Don't get down until you have finished your dinner." Her voice was also the voice of direction in terms of relationships: "Don't let that get to you, Anne"; "Forgive and try to forget"; "Go and find someone else to play with"; and, the best of all, "Let's pray about it." It wasn't that Anne's dad wasn't great, but that her mum was the one who was around the most. Her voice has been one of the most influential in Anne's life and she will always be grateful for her. We can have all kinds of people trying to take us in all kinds of directions, and the older Anne gets, the more she realizes the value of parents whose voices were pointing her to Jesus.

But then there was a moment with her mum that changed her life forever.

Anne called her mum regularly after getting married and they would have lovely chats. But there was one conversation that shifted her thinking entirely. Anne was, as usual, asking advice on a bunch of things, and she clearly recalls her mum saying, "Anne, have you spoken to Gavin about this?" and Anne thought, "No, I am talking to you!" Her mum went on, "I think you need to go to him first; you are married now." At the time it was painful for Anne. It felt like a total rejection. Twenty-two years of going to her mum, seeking her advice, sharing her heart, trusting her voice above the rest, and it felt like it was all ending in one phone chat.

Anne got on her knees that day and wept with pain and loss. It may sound strange, but it totally rattled her. It wasn't that she didn't want to share with Gavin; it was just that her mum had always been the one whom she talked to about the deep stuff. Something huge shifted in our marriage after that conversation, an amazing intimacy began, and Anne started to understand what "leaving and cleaving" really, truly meant. We opened our hearts to one another in a whole new way and a new journey began.

However, this was not the most significant thing that came out of Anne's conversation with her mum. After they had spoken, when she was down on her knees, broken and weeping, Anne encountered Jesus. It wasn't that she didn't know Him; it was that she saw Him in a whole new way. In the face of knowing that it perhaps wasn't the best idea to depend on a human being like she was with her mum, she began to understand that Jesus wanted her to look to Him. She sensed His arms around her that afternoon. She realized that His love for her extended to any place. Anywhere. Anytime. Anne's true dependency on Christ began on that day. Her ability to hear the voice of Jesus, through the power of the Holy Spirit, took on a whole new level from that point onwards.

What her mum said that day was painful for her too, but it was for the best. They have a beautiful relationship now, a mutually less dependent one, and the ability to spur one another on in their relationships with Jesus. Anne thanks God for what her mum said because it birthed a greater intimacy in her marriage and in her walk with the Lord of the universe.

WHOSE VOICE IS THE LOUDEST?

We wonder **what voices are the loudest in your life**. Who governs and guides the decisions that you make and the way that you live daily? We are all formed and shaped by those who have raised us, but is their voice so loud that we have confused it with the voice of the King? We know for us there are so many moments when the voices of friends, the insights of reason, and the views of those with more experience can often drown out the voice of God.

When the Egyptians were chasing the Israelites towards the Red Sea, they were following the voice of Pharaoh. His voice was the loudest sound of all, and they were led by it, dictated to by it, and consumed by it. The very notion of them "hearing God" in the midst of that mayhem was – although not impossible – extremely tough. The Egyptians would have grown up believing from a young age that the Israelites were their property – they were "meant to be" enslaved to them, they belonged to them, and the Egyptians were in charge. How dare the Israelites try to escape? We will show them the real truth – their God can't really save them.

What is fascinating is what happens in front of them as they pursue the Israelites towards the Red Sea:

The angel of God, who had been travelling in front of Israel's army, withdrew and went behind them. The pillar of cloud also moved from in front and stood behind them, coming between the armies of Egypt

*and Israel. Throughout the night the cloud brought
darkness to the one side and light to the other; so
neither went near the other all night long (Exodus
14:19–20).*

Listening to the voice of Pharaoh leads us to a cloudy, dark
place, where we cannot see the way ahead. Listening and
following the Lord's voice keeps us in a place of light and
safety, with hope ahead. We can think that we are listening
to the right voices, but they are human and conditional;
however great they may be, they are nothing compared to
the voice of God.

What happens next is truly incredible: the Israelites
watch in wonder as Moses stretches his hand over the sea
and a mighty wind blows back the water so that they can
walk through on dry land, with walls of water on either side
(Exodus 14:21–22). We wonder how long the cloud obscured
the Egyptians' view of this magnificent sight. We know they
began to pursue the Israelites, but had they seen the Lord
split the sea? Had they followed the wrong voice so much
and become so clouded in their vision that they were unable
to see the Lord perform this incredible act? Scary to think
that listening to the wrong voices can stop us seeing the Lord
move in miraculous ways.

When we stop and think about the cloud for a minute,
we are able to consider more fully the way that it prevented
the Egyptians from seeing and hearing what the Lord God
Almighty was doing. When thick cloud covers the skies, we
are totally unaware of the warmth and light of the sun. We
do not see anything as clearly as we would when the cloud
is pushed away, and when it is present it can make us feel
heavy, lethargic, and narrower in perspective. If you fly in an
aeroplane up and through the clouds, suddenly you meet a

bright blue sky and a shining sun – it looks as if the sky goes on forever. However, as you fly through the thick cloud, you wonder when it will clear and where you are going.

WHAT IS YOUR CLOUD?

Picturing the Egyptians with the cloud in front of them, we visualize ourselves and wonder what stands between God and us. What cloud have we allowed to form in front of our lives, so that we are unable to see the glory of the Lord, to enter into what the Spirit is doing and saying to us, and to walk forward in freedom?

Anne recalls going for a run on holiday and crying out to God, asking, "Why do you feel so far away? What are you saying to me? I don't feel like I can hear you!" She had prayed all the good Christian prayers but He still seemed distant. Anne found that, as she ran, she became aware of some fear in her life. It started with realizing that she was afraid of not finding the right way back to the apartment we were staying in. She decided it was best to stay on the main road and not turn off it but just do a U-turn when she had gone halfway. At this point Anne became aware that this was how she was living her life – sticking to the obvious route, the protected way, the simple path, because she was afraid of what could happen if she tried something new or pushed out of the boundaries. This revelation led her to prayers of repentance for not trusting God, and then a deep sense of His presence came. She could see a wall in front of her – she was bashing it down and moving the bricks out of the way – then she was able to see Jesus and she knew the way ahead. Fear had been like a cloud obliterating her view of Christ and stopping her from stepping out and growing in her relationship with God. As Henri Nouwen beautifully states, "**Fear is the great enemy**

of intimacy. Fear makes us run away from each other or cling to each other but it does not create true intimacy." Anne ran lots of different routes on that holiday and felt as free as a bird. She knew Jesus was close to her. She then came home and began to explore ordination.

So many things can be like that cloud, stopping us from hearing the voice of God and having the faith to walk forward into freedom. We don't want to miss what the Spirit is doing, because we are blinded by our own selfish pursuits. One of our all-time favourite life stories is that of William Wilberforce and his journey to try to better society. What an incredible man, overcoming his own personal issues, and not stopping until he metaphorically saw the seas part and the slave trade end. We love it when he says, "We are too young to realise that certain things are impossible… so we will do them anyway." The clouds in his life – his illness, his age, his nightmares, and his faith held in tension with his political success – did not prevent him from walking with Jesus and fulfilling His call on his life. The film *Amazing Grace* portrays Wilberforce as having a very real battle with whether he can be a political activist as well as having a living faith. His young Prime Minister friend William Pitt says to him, "Do you intend to use that beautiful voice to praise the Lord or change the world?" Wilberforce became so aware of his weaknesses, but yet they did not cloud his vision so much that he stopped doing what God had for him to do. He praised the Lord and changed the world!

Our view of ourselves can also be like a huge thick cloud, stopping us from seeing God's mighty hand opening up the sea in front of us. We can find that we are either full of pride or full of self-doubt. The Egyptians were very sure of themselves; they thought that they could "outrun" and "outdo" God. Even after all the plagues they were willing to follow the Israelites into the sea, believing that they could be victorious! Crazy that sometimes we think that we know better than anyone, even God, and that our plan, our way, is the best. They say that pride comes before a fall, and boy this was a mighty fall for the Egyptian army.

And yet self-doubt hangs like a destructive, restrictive cloud too. We cannot count the number of people we have seen begin to push out into what God may be asking them to do, and then give up or pull back a bit because they doubt themselves and think that they are too sinful or not good enough to do it. Whenever we find ourselves in a place of thinking negatively about what we are doing or who we are, it hangs like a cloud over our lives and it is very difficult to hear the voice of God.

Jesus does not want us to focus on the sin, but be liberated from it. As the Lord's Prayer vitally reminds us to pray, "Father forgive us our sin, as we forgive those who sin against us." Our mess does not equal who we are. **Our past does not define our future**. We can let it remain there like a dark cloud, or we can seek forgiveness, know that the slate is clean, and walk fully and freely into our future.

As a teenager Anne remembers a holiday camp where one of the leaders wrote in her Bible, "Anne, remember JOY", and she thought she just struggled to write a full sentence, but she followed it with "… put nothing between Jesus and yourself." Extremely cheesy we know; however, as a thirteen-year-old, it meant a lot to Anne. So many things can come between us and Jesus, stopping us from hearing and seeing Him. The Prodigal Son lets his desire for "life on his terms" prevent him from having a relationship with God, and his choices create a huge distance between them. We could say that the older brother remains close to his father – this is true in terms of physical distance. However, you could argue that the older brother's feelings towards his father in relation to his younger brother create as big a distance between them.

Our feelings, thoughts, and actions are in desperate need of the grace and love of our God! In reflecting on the Prodigal Son narrative, Henri Nouwen considers the distance we create between us and Jesus: "I am so afraid of being disliked, blamed, put aside, passed over, ignored, persecuted, and killed that I am constantly developing strategies to defend myself and therefore assure myself of the love I think I need and deserve. And in so doing I move far away from my father's home and choose to dwell in a distant country."[1]

There is a need to keep returning to the Father, to keep seeking out the Spirit's guiding voice and asking Him to break through our messy cloud of humanness so that we can see the Son again; to know God's whisper in our deepest being and be prepared to listen to it.

DON'T LISTEN TO THE WRONG VOICES!

Some of our problem is that as the cloud descends and we lose sight of God and His voice, we can begin to listen to the wrong voices. As we clamber around in the chaotic darkness, not sure where to go, other voices can take us off on a tangent and confuse our thinking and our focus. Nouwen helpfully reflects on these voices:

> *They are always there and always, they reach into those inner places where I question my own goodness and doubt my self-worth. They suggest that I am not going to be loved without my having earned it through determined efforts and hard work. They want me to prove to myself and others that I am worth being loved, and they keep pushing me to do everything possible to gain acceptance. They deny loudly that love is a total free gift. I leave home every time I lose faith in the voice that calls me the beloved*

and follow the voices that offer a great variety of
ways to win the love I so much desire. [2]

The wrong voices can be present in all kinds of contexts, and it's important we don't listen to them and end up with the wrong outcome. As British children of the eighties and early nineties it's impossible for us to not remember the concept of a "Kodak moment". This advertising slogan summed up the technology of the day, in which photos were taken on a film, then sent away and returned with varying degrees of quality some weeks later. Kodak had the world at their feet and were seen as technology and innovation at its best. However, this was really not the case.

By 1976 Kodak accounted for 90 per cent of film and 85 per cent of camera sales in the USA, and in the 1990s was regularly rated as one of the world's five most valuable brands. However, before any of this, back in 1975 (a long time before the digital age) Kodak had built one of the first digital cameras.[3] This posed a problem. If digital technology developed then this would put their core business of print under threat. David Usborne wrote in *The Independent* that "for Kodak's leaders, going digital meant killing film, smashing the company's golden egg to make way for the new".[4] So, at the time that Sony were releasing the first digital camera, Kodak researched and discovered that the "good" news was that it would take some time for things to catch on and they had roughly ten years to prepare for the transition to digital so could stick with printing.[5]

The end of the story is that Kodak's international business is in tatters, many others have taken their place in the market, and the company is left with very little – all because they chose to play it safe, listened to the voices of caution, and failed to innovate. They chose death over innovation! We hope and pray that the same will never be true for the church, that being over cautious will never take over, and that we will be prepared to take risks, reimagine things, and challenge the status quo both inside and outside the church – that we will not miss the voice of God because we chose to hear the voice of safety.

God, please let our humanness decrease that your holiness would increase! There is a longing that we would see a bigger picture than what we naturally see, so that we are awakened to the voice of God and His view of us. We love the way Jesus speaks to Mary and Martha, reminding them of what is important. **Mary is listening to Jesus, whilst Martha is rushing around, and yet He wants both of them to sit at His feet** (Luke 10:38–42). The King of the world has so much to say to us, to reveal to us, to involve us in; we just need to begin to discern His voice – to give Him time and space in our crazy busy lives… that we may not have a "Kodak moment" of our own.

YES! But how?

YOU AND GOD

Looking at me:

How about us? Are we able to hear the Lord and see what He is doing, or is there a cloud in front of us, just like the Egyptians experienced between them and the Israelites?

Why not pray for clarity – for Jesus to show you anything that stands between you and Him, and for Him to knock it down so that you can draw near to Him again.

Check out the "How does God guide us?" suggestions from the Alpha course (Session 7 – you can look up the talk online):

Guidance can look like: Commanding Scripture, Compelling Spirit, Common Sense, Counsel of Saints, Circumstantial Signs.

Looking back:

Think back to a time when you were looking for guidance from God. Did you think you had it? What was the outcome? Looking back, did you make the right decision? Are there times when you think you did not act in line with God's best plan? What could you have done differently? Let's learn from how the Lord has led us before.

Listen:

"At the Foot of the Cross", by One Hundred Hours, from their album *Lift*. (You may be able to access this online.)

GROUP ACTIVITY

Looking at the big picture:

In so many places around the world Christians are suffering persecution and struggling to continue walking in the footsteps of Jesus, to follow after His voice, rather than the voice of those around them. Just like the Israelites, being pursued to the Red Sea by the Egyptians, Christians all over the world are being chased out of their homes, persecuted, isolated, and living in poverty and fear.

This persecution of Christians worldwide has become such a significant issue that Release International, Open Doors, Christian Solidarity Worldwide, and the Evangelical Alliance have joined together to form the Religious Liberty Commission.

The **Religious Liberty Commission** (RLC) exists to speak up for Christians who are persecuted because of their faith. While it has this specific mandate to speak up for Christians, it strongly believes in the rights of all people, of any faith or none, to have freedom of religion or belief, including the freedom to convert. Further info can be found here: www.eauk.org/church/networks/religious-liberty-commission/

Why not take a look at the **Open Doors** website and pray for our brothers and sisters: www.opendoorsuk.org/persecution/country_profiles.php

Looking closer to home:

The church here may not be persecuted in the same way as the church in Africa, China, and the Middle East (to name a few places), but it is becoming increasingly challenging, as the world becomes more secularized, to hear the voice of the Lord and walk in Spirit and truth.

Why not take a look at the **Evangelical Alliance** website and pray for our church to stand strong: www.eauk.org/church/research-and-statistics/

Further reading

N. Gumbel, *How Does God Guide Us?* (Eastbourne: Kingsway Publications, 2003)

D. Tidball, *How Does God Guide? Help to Discern God's Will for Your Life* (Fearn: Christian Focus, 2001)

12
Transforming Our Communities

"Change happens because people don't give up, they don't take no for an answer, they keep demanding change."

ED MILIBAND

The quote above was given by the outgoing Labour party leader Ed Miliband, on Friday 8 May 2015, during his resignation speech the day after his party had suffered a crushing defeat in the UK General Election. In the face of such a failing there remained a need to press on and keep going; otherwise, in his eyes, nothing would ever improve or change. It sums up the need for human spirit in bringing about change. It won't always be quick and it might not always come easy. Change sometimes takes tenacity on behalf of those seeking it. It requires a "can do" mentality and a desire to press on. The need for spiritual change in the UK is clear, but are we prepared to stand up for it and keep demanding it?

We have considered how we *listen* to the right voice and begin to respond to the voice of the Lord more in our lives, but now we need to ask the question, "How in this world can we *be* the right voice?" However challenging the landscape looks, we remain wholeheartedly convinced that it's through the church that this nation will be transformed. After all, it's only Christ that can provide hope to the hopeless, a family to the lonely and isolated, and restoration to the broken. We the church are His bride, called to be His hands and feet, and His ambassadors, activists, and workers in our communities.

THE CHANGING FACE OF BRITAIN

For many hundreds of years, the church in Britain was the very epicentre of the community. Every town and village had a church. Going to church on a Sunday was seen as important, beneficial, and edifying to both the individual and the wider community. There was a clear social benefit to going too. It was the "done" thing to attend church. Additionally, the church school was a good place to educate your children, and Sunday school would provide the next generation with a well-rounded and wholesome worldview. Stories such as Jonah being swallowed by a great fish (Jonah 1), the walls of Jericho falling down (Joshua 6), and Paul being blinded on the road to Damascus (Acts 9), were well known and accepted.

Many may argue that such days were a lifetime ago, and that this is all over-the-top Christian hyperbole, but that simply isn't the case. It's only been a generation or two since church buildings were exclusively used for housing worshipping congregations. Today in Britain old churches can often be seen functioning as carpet warehouses, flash wine bars, and squatter communities, but that was not always the case. The former England football captain and global sporting icon David Beckham was a regular attendee in his childhood. He says, "I was playing football with the Cubs as well, which you could only do if you went to church on Sunday. So all the family – me, mum and dad and my sisters – made sure we were there every time without fail."[1] Just a generation or so ago, when Beckham was a lad, there were social benefits in going to church.

Whether we like it or not, the church no longer holds the same position in our society. Today it has lost this place and, if anything, has been usurped by the school and education. The former British Schools Minister David Miliband made the point some years ago that the school had to fill the void left by the church at the very heart of our communities. The fundamental problem is that the church no longer attracts people as it used to do. There simply aren't as many people going through the doors on a Sunday as there once were. Today the previously well-known and loved Bible stories that dominated childhoods seem little more than myth, and the name of Jesus is just a swear word to so many. Lots of people only see the church as worthwhile when it becomes a location for their picture book wedding. We are living in what is an ever more secularized society.

Within this changing landscape the church can seem so out of place too. We talk of the greatest revolutionary of all time, who walked the planet giving food to the hungry (John 6), sight to the blind (John 9), and life to the dead (John 11), and yet too often all that our world sees is old buildings, vicars wearing dresses, pastors who ignore current realities, and caveman beliefs unthinkingly adopted by the majority of the faithful. Now we know this is not true, but people's perception of reality can quickly take over from the truth itself; we the people of God need to take some ownership for how Christianity is seen in our nation.

CHANGE IS NEEDED!

So we are left in little doubt that change is needed. We can no longer simply accept the status quo and be tolerant of the fact that Christianity is dwindling in the UK. Globally the church is exploding at an incredible rate, but here it's increasingly seen as yesterday's news. It's perceived as the faith of the older generations, the establishment, and of a day gone by. Spirituality itself is in vogue but the church is the one spiritual thing that's often seen as entirely irrelevant. In our incessantly politically correct world Christianity remains one thing that people don't mind having a go at. Just the other day our daughter came back quite upset from primary school. She had been mocked that day for her faith. She's the only Christian in her class, but there are many kids from other faiths. She gets teased because what could be more odd and strange to her young friends than for her to follow Christ? This has got to change.

We read an interesting article written in response to the Belfast-based Ashers Bakers, which was found to have discriminated against a customer for refusing to supply a cake with the slogan "Support Gay Marriage". In it the pro-gay marriage writer says something very illuminating: "Britain is rightly proud of being a nation that tolerates all religions and beliefs. And while that tolerance is afforded to many religions, it's clear not much of it wings its way into the Christian camp."[2] It was so encouraging to hear someone say that Christians can "get a bad rap in this country", not so that we can lie down and try to make ourselves feel better, but be aware of the situation we find ourselves in and not be afraid to be true to what we believe.

What then do we need in place in order to see cultural transformation for Christ? American writer and president of the organization Marketplace Leaders, Os Hillman, says that "culture is shaped by the seven mountains of cultural influence – business, government, media, arts and entertainment, family, education and the church".[3] We as Christians need to be influencing, or better still leading, within these seven areas. We can't afford to just stick to church, for that is but one of the seven. In order to transform our communities, and moreover our nation, we need Christians making a difference in each of these places.

We as a church need to learn to support people in these other areas too. It's easy to know what's needed to support an overseas missionary with their financial needs and regular prayer letters, but **how do we as Christians help business leaders living for Christ?** How can we stop bemoaning the methods of the media and instead infiltrate them? Arts and entertainment are fields that desperately need Christian presence, and as for family and education these are historically real strongpoints for the church. In our local congregation we wonder how many of the seven mountains of cultural influence are represented in our church and how well we are doing at supporting people in these areas. We must start validating, endorsing, and supporting people seeking to bring the light and love of Christ into environments of influence beyond the walls of the church.

So, as well as the areas of influence, what kind of people are needed in order to make real change? What constitutes a game changer? In his book *The Catalyst Leader* Brad Lomenick outlines eight characteristics that are required to become a change maker. These are 1) Calling (finding out God's unique plan for your life); 2) Authenticity (being the person you are meant to be at all times and sharing this with others); 3) Passion (for life and your relationship with God); 4) Capable (growing your gift set and being up to achieving high standards); 5) Courageous (learning to push through and take risks. Being able to manage your fears not be stopped by them); 6) Principled (based in clearly held views and principles); 7) Hopeful (optimistic about a brighter future);

8) Collaborative (someone who will work with others towards the greater good).[4]

How many of these characteristics do you find yourself naturally carrying? Are there some you need to work on or pray that the Lord might gift you in? Perhaps there are others around you who can fill in the gaps for you and vice versa. After all we are a body.

MISSION AT ALL TIMES

We the UK church really need to value mission that takes place in all areas of society. We will only influence an entire culture by impacting the various aspects of it. In particular, we believe that we need to begin recognizing and affirming more strongly mission to others taking place in informal settings and relationships. We the church are forever looking for volunteers to help with jobs within the building, from the flower rota to the youth group. There is nothing wrong with this; however, we need to release people to not be "busy being busy" on numerous internal church commitments but instead to be free to be Jesus in their community.

Jesus used everyday meetings with people, and often in one-on-one situations, to share His message. A good example is found in John 3, when Nicodemus comes to meet Jesus secretly during the night. There was no pomp and ceremony and no great religious festival, just a private encounter and a conversation. We must seek to encourage, and develop, a church in which one of the most important things we do is sharing the Lord in love through our everyday lives. When did you last hear a sermon on sharing your faith at work? Or communicating Jesus in the supermarket? Or witnessing over a pint of beer in a pub? Or a coffee in Starbucks? These are exactly the kinds of situations that the church needs to be addressing and encouraging.

We need to mobilize our people into action. We must take seriously our links to the world. We have to reach out to others. We are compelled to be amongst those whom no one else loves. Why? Because that is where our Jesus would be. Who is there in your community that no one loves? What might your church do for these folks? What are the key issues in your community that no one is doing anything about, and how might you and your church begin to address these things? How can we take on issues that we see, whilst making it clear that we are doing it in the name of Jesus? The church has a rich history of an entrepreneurial heart and approach to social needs, from provision of education and availability of healthcare, to the abolition of the slave trade. What is going on in your community that's wrong and needs standing up to? Let's not just be conscientious objectors who make it clear what we don't like, or approve of; let's be people who actually change things. In the famous words of Mahatma Gandhi, **"Be the change that you wish to see in the world."** There are many organizations and resources that can help you with some of this and we are pleased to list a few at the end of this chapter.

The question "**If you were put on trial for being a Christian, would there be enough evidence to convict you?**" remains an incredibly strong challenge today. Does the life you live show clear signs of the God you are living for? In your everyday situation, amongst those you work with, in your family home, when out in your community, when driving your car, when you haven't slept well the night before, when someone else is rude to you – in all of these situations is there evidence for you living a life for Jesus? Do you talk about Him, as well as try to live like Him? We all need to start living in a way that is no longer confined to church and is out there amongst the people sharing the message of Jesus.

Putting on a good performance of Christianity amongst our fellow Christians is not enough – we need to do our utmost to live for Jesus all the time in word and in deed. Yes, we'll make mistakes, but His grace is sufficient for us (2 Corinthians 12:9), and we have the fantastic promise that He is with us always (Matthew 28:20). In other words, Jesus requires every sinew of our being, capacity of our brain, energy in our bodies, and devotion of our hearts. If we corporately did this then it wouldn't take as much as we might think to change the world.

The task so often seems impossible but the picture is not as bleak as we are led to believe. We have incredible resources at our disposal, a loyal and vibrant bunch of Christians, facilities in every community, and most importantly a God who can move mountains on our side. Compared with the humble beginnings of our Lord and the often lacklustre youth group He started out with (we usually call them the disciples!) we are in an incredible position. That lot didn't do too badly after Jesus ascended either! We need to be hopeful, Spirit-filled believers who are prepared to take on this nation in the name of Jesus.

We were hugely encouraged, and equally challenged, by some recent research from the Barna group (find more at www.talkingjesus.org) that showed that 66 per cent of

UK Christians have shared their faith in the last month.[5] Disappointingly, however, 42 per cent of those shared with felt glad that they didn't share the Christians faith, and a further 42 per cent felt indifferent as a result.[6] We are desperately hoping that we would keep sharing as prolifically, but that the impact would be immensely more positive.

The stark numbers and facts themselves are not too bad. **If every Christian in Britain helped one person a week to find faith, it would take just one month for the whole nation to become Christian**. This is both surprising and encouraging. If we can help every Christian to share their faith, then the West could follow parts of Asia, Latin America, and Africa in falling on its knees before the King of kings. We need a church where there is enough evidence to convict every last one of us. This way we could change our communities, workplaces, and schools. We could see the church back at the heart of the community. We would be more dangerous and the world could no longer ignore us and think nothing of our mission. Surely the future has to look like this – the alternative is terrifying. The only other option is that we stay locked away, hiding our light, rather than rescuing the masses who never go near church!

MOST IMPORTANTLY OF ALL… PRAY!

For all that's written above about transforming our communities, if we were only going to do one thing then that should be to pray. Every major move of God is saturated in prayer. Reading through the major revivals and renewals in church history, there is always a huge foundation of prayer underpinning all that is going on. We are sometimes so focused on activism that we forget to stop and pray. Our efforts will be so less impactful if not supported and upheld in prayer. The great American writer Philip Yancey puts it this way: "Prayer may seem at first like disengagement, a reflective time to consider God's point of view. But that vantage presses us back to accomplish God's will, the work of the kingdom. We are God's fellow workers, and as such we turn to prayer to equip us for the partnership."[7]

Our work will be ill-equipped without the undergirding of prayer. Moreover, our mission and the transformation of our communities will also significantly lack power without prayer behind it. The inspiring leader in this area of prayer, Pete Greig, writes, "I am convinced, however, that our constant activity is fruitless without first making that humble act of kneeling to pray. I am convinced that prayer is not only our greatest privilege, but also our greatest source of power."[8] All that we do, and are, must revolve around a commitment to a lifestyle of prayer.

The time Jesus spends praying in Gethsemane (Matthew 26:36–46) teaches us a lot about prayer and how we should approach it. First, we see the utter necessity of prayer. Regardless of what we are dealing with we simply cannot approach it without prayer. Jesus is about to face the cross, so what does He do? He prays. Second, we learn about the value of repeated prayer. Jesus prays three times for the same thing. He prays with all He has that the suffering lying ahead of him might be removed. Instead of praying once and quitting, Jesus teaches the need to petition and repeat our prayers. Third, we learn about the utter mystery of unanswered prayer. Even Jesus, the Son of God, does not get His prayer answered in the way He wants. We must pray, but we must be open to the fact that, though heard, our requests will not necessarily be answered in the affirmative.[9] As we take transforming our communities seriously, we must too be praying, be doing so repeatedly, and be open to the fact we won't always hear what we want to!

As we pray we need to also be aware that this may change our lives entirely! Back in 2006 Adrian Curtis and his family were at Spring Harvest and their whole world changed. Adrian writes:

My wife and I had felt God beginning to birth in us a heart for people in crisis and poverty. We knew God was calling us to something and whilst we sat in our chalet together we prayed a dangerous prayer. We prayed that God would show us during Spring Harvest what He wanted us to do. We promised God that we would do whatever He asked; if He wanted us to move house, sell our house, leave our jobs we were willing to give it all up for Him. We went to the evening meeting afterwards. The speaker challenged us to examine if we were worshipping the real Jesus or a version of Jesus that suited our comfort zone. The real Jesus told the rich young ruler to give up everything and give it to the poor. What the preacher said cut us to our hearts to the point we could no longer speak any words to each other. In a daze we wandered back to the Skyline for a coffee, and my wife and I both recognized that we needed to leave our jobs, get out of the boat, and step out in faith.

When we returned from Spring Harvest my wife resigned from her job the next day. She had been working for a bank and eventually found work for a charity. To be completely honest I lacked faith and didn't resign straight away. I did look into poverty statistics for my area and whilst praying one day for God to show me what He wanted me to do, the word "Foodbank" dropped into my mind. I googled it and found The Trussell Trust. Through our small church which was still running in South Wales I launched Wales' first Trussell Trust Foodbank in 2008, one of then only 26 in the UK. Still lacking the faith to totally resign from my role, I decided to put one foot out of the boat and went part time to volunteer my time to establish the Foodbank. Later that year God had clearly had enough of my lack of faith and decided to give me a nudge out of the boat – I was made redundant! The Trussell Trust employed me for two days per week to help other churches develop foodbanks in Wales. I became the first Foodbank Regional Development Officer in 2009 and the first Regional Manager for Wales in 2011. In 2013 the Foodbank Director retired and I was employed as the National Director.

As a result of their dangerous prayer asking God what to do and being prepared to do whatever the answer required, Adrian now oversees a network of over 1,200 local Foodbank centres. Last year the thousands of churches and 30,000 volunteers in this network fed nearly 1,000,000 people. This is one of the largest church-led social action initiatives in the UK that is quite literally shaping our nation. Prayer leads to change and this is what transforms a community!

We want to be game changers. The landscape needs changing; we are all on a mission, and most importantly of all, we need to harness and undergird the whole thing with prayer. God is a God of transformation. For evidence of that just look at your own life! He wants us involved in changing our communities. Perhaps it's time you prayed a dangerous prayer too, asking the Lord quite what it is that He wants to use you for in order to make a real impact in the area you live in and the places that you find yourself. In the words of Isaiah, maybe it's time we started to say meaningfully to the Lord that whatever He wants to do in our community our cry in return is simply, "Here am I. Send me!" (Isaiah 6:8).

YES! But how?

YOU AND GOD

There are seven mountains of influence in culture...

In the mid-seventies God gave Bill Bright (founder of Campus Crusade), Loren Cunningham (founder of Youth with a Mission), and Francis Schaeffer a shared vision for cultural transformation. The vision was simple but profound. In order to transform any nation for Jesus the people of God had to impact and affect all seven cultural mountains (or spheres) of that society.

Those seven mountains are business, government, media, arts and entertainment, education, the family, and religion. There are many subgroups under these main categories.

www.7culturalmountains.org/

Which mountain (or subgroup) do you have an influence in?

1. Business
2. Government
3. Media
4. Arts and entertainment
5. Education
6. Family
7. Religion

How can you take Jesus into your area of influence? Through conversation, through action, through prayer? What is He asking you to do? Remember that you join with thousands of brothers and sisters seeking to show the love of Jesus and take His truth into the places that they influence.

GROUP ACTIVITY

1. Considering the mountains of influence above, identify
    each area, asking those listening to stand if they operate in
    the first, second, third, etc. When those in "Business" are
    standing, try to gather them together so that they can see
    that they are not alone; then those around can lay hands
    on them and really pray for the Lord's anointing on their
    ministry in the workplace, that He would bless them and
    use them in greater measure for His glory! Do the same
    with all seven mountains, then ask anyone who hasn't
    stood to stand and pray for them (there may be areas that
    haven't been covered).

2. How can the group "be the right voice" where they are?
    Perhaps they feel hopeless about talking about God.
    Maybe they lack faith or confidence, or feel ill-equipped.
    Encourage them that if we step out God will give them
    what they need. As Peter walked on water and began to
    sink, the Lord took hold of his hand. He will ultimately
    grow us and strengthen us; we just have to get out of the
    boat. Pray for those who feel lacking. Invite the Holy
    Spirit to come and touch them and empower them afresh.
    There may well be some dreams/underlying thoughts
    buried with a lot of excuses in people's lives. Ask the Lord
    to remind them of where He wants them to be the right
    voice, or to plant new dreams in their hearts and minds.
    Pray that they will come into being.

Some tools for prayer

www.24-7prayer.com/helpmepray
www.worldprayer.org.uk/wpc-resources
www.trypraying.org/your-prayer/

Some tools for reaching others

www.alpha.org

www.christianityexplored.org

www.thepublicleader.com

Just 10 (Available from www.canonjjohn.com/just10)

Sharing Jesus: How to put your faith into words (Available from www.sharejesusinternational.com)

Stepping into Evangelism (Available from www.churcharmy. org.uk)

The Crazy Way, Christian Vision for Men (Available from www.cwr.org.uk)

The Heartbeat of Mission (Available from www.hopetogether. org.uk)

The Natural Evangelism Course (Available from www. canonjjohn.com/store/books)

Your job. God's Work (Available from www.licc.org.uk)

For youth specifically: *Hope Revolution Chatterbox* (Available from www.hopetogether.org.uk/Groups/258874/Chatterbox_ Fun_size.aspx)

Further reading

L. Singlehurst, *Sowing. Reaping, Keeping* (Nottingham, IVP, 2006)

P. Yancey, *Prayer: Does it make any difference?* (London: Hodder & Stoughton, 2008)

Part 5

EMPOWER

Deuteronomy 34:1 – Joshua 1:11

13
Passing the Baton

"I need willing hands to accept the torch for a new generation."

BILLY GRAHAM

Wedged amongst four hundred sweaty teenagers, Anne sat on the sticky carpet, listening open mouthed to the young female preacher on the stage. The preacher filled the stage with energy, life, and passion. You could have heard a pin drop; she held her crowd so well. Sharing her experience of walking with Jesus and giving the young people humorous and insightful anecdotes to help them to walk with Him too, she captivated the crowd with her anointing and confidence. It was twenty minutes that Anne will remember forever. She was struggling to hold the tears back – not eyes wet with sadness, but soggy with pride and joy. Here she was, seven years on from the day that she first met the girl, who was now on the stage preaching at a hugely respected Christian conference, to hundreds of eleven- to fourteen-year-olds and totally transformed by the power and the love of Christ.

Anne sat there reflecting on the journey that this preacher girl had taken – one that she knew in her heart had amazed both of them. In Anne's mind she could still picture an eighteen-year-old girl knocking on our door, trembling with nerves and unsure of what to say. A good friend of ours and her youth pastor at the time had asked Anne if she would mentor this girl and she had readily agreed. Anne knew the girl was special, even though it would be a long journey of getting her to realize and believe it for herself. They had chatted for a couple of hours that first day, Anne listening to her story and slowly and sensitively building a relationship. Over time Anne learnt of family life broken at a very young age, of a very poorly mum whom she had quickly learnt to look after, and of a very tight knit unit that included her grandma and stepdad. Anne went on to discover how she and her one sibling had dragged their mum, who had a few months to live, to a local healing meeting and had seen her be miraculously healed from cancer in her blood. Some humour lay in the fact that her mum's partner had bought her a brand new Audi TT to enjoy in the last few months of life – however, when she defied all medical understanding and continued living, he had to insist on taking it back because they couldn't afford it! Anne began to see glimpses through the shy and nervous exterior of a girl who knew that God was real and who believed that He could do the impossible. The challenge was to help her to realize that He could do these incredible things in and through her life too.

Over time she has begun to see herself as God sees her. Anne has had the privilege of watching her confidence grow, of seeing her mature into an incredibly strong woman who knows that God is calling her to do great things in His name and for His kingdom (despite, like the rest of us, doubting it sometimes). She is committed to mentoring other girls, from challenging backgrounds, so that they can grow into all God wants them to be. She has taken hold of her passion for troubled people and is serving Jesus in trying to see them be set free. We are both excited to see how the next stage of her journey unfolds!

As Anne compared the scared, shivering eighteen-year-old on our front doorstep to the confident, capable twenty-five-year-old on the stage in front of her, she found it truly remarkable. God is in the business of changing lives in ways that we never dreamt or imagined possible. Jesus was showing Anne that when we take time to invest who we are into others, they can go so much further than we would ever dream of going. This is the work of the kingdom: not going it alone to achieve personal goals, but to share our experiences, to open up opportunities, and to encourage others on, so that they can carry Christ and His mission on beyond us.

As Anne came back to reality on the carpet, surrounded by transfixed young people staring at the stage, she felt a deep inner glow – a sense of thankfulness that God would use her in this way, but more than that, that He would allow her the privilege of seeing this young woman transform before her eyes. Our prayer is that she will see even greater things than we will see and make such a deep impact for the kingdom.

MENTORING RELATIONSHIPS

When we think about mentoring relationships like this, we cannot help but be drawn into 1 and 2 Kings and the story of Elijah and Elisha. What an incredible example of living "life on life" – sharing experiences, watching, learning, listening, and modelling a powerful walk with God. The story begins in 1 Kings 19:19–21, where Elijah throws his cloak around

Elisha and he thus leaves his home, slaughters his oxen, and becomes Elijah's assistant. Elisha has no idea what this decision will mean for the rest of his life; following Elijah and learning from him leads him to a place of leadership that he never dreamt or imagined.

When we get to 2 Kings 2 we are at the end of Elijah's life, and the Lord is about to take him up to heaven. They are in the company of fifty prophets and Elijah asks Elisha, "What can I do for you before I am taken from you?" Elisha replies, "Let me inherit a double portion of your spirit" (2:9). Scripturally we know that the rights of the firstborn meant that they would receive a "double portion" of everything belonging to the Father (Deuteronomy 21:17) – therefore being given double the inheritance of any of the other sons. Elisha, as Elijah's spiritual successor, is effectively asking for more of God, in order to continue the work that Elijah has been doing. He wants "special privileges as his master's successor, possibly as leader of the community of prophets".[1]

Then an incredible moment unfolds before his eyes, making him able to take on the mantle from Elijah (2:10–12); a chariot of fire and horses of fire appear and Elijah goes up to heaven in a whirlwind. Elisha then takes his master's cloak, strikes the water, and sees it move to the right and to the left. The prophets acknowledge, "The Spirit of Elijah is resting on Elisha", and they bow down before him (2:15). The mantle is passed on to Elisha to continue the Lord's work, with a double portion of blessing.

This is Anne's prayer for her mentee – not that she would watch Anne go up to heaven in a chariot (although that sounds pretty awesome!) but that she would inherit more than her, that she would go on to do greater things for Jesus than Anne has seen and done, and that she would have double the anointing and blessing that Anne has had in following Christ.

Life is short and we need spiritual younger people whom we keep investing in, to know the power of the Spirit on their lives and take the gospel further, reaching more with the truth, so that eternity is filled with many more transformed souls.

We see a story of mentoring and succession with Moses and Joshua too. However, in their story we do not witness Joshua picking up a cloak and splitting the water but Moses publicly affirming that he is to lead the people forward: "Be strong and courageous, for you must go with this people into the land that the Lord swore to their ancestors to give them, and you must divide it among them as their inheritance. The Lord himself goes before you and will be with you; he will never leave you nor forsake you. Do not be afraid; do not be discouraged" (Deuteronomy 31:7–8). Joshua does not ask for a double portion, but Moses affirms that the Lord is with him, and we know that he was "filled with the Spirit of wisdom because Moses had laid his hands on him" (Deuteronomy 34:9).

We stand in wonder of Moses, questioning whether he struggled with commissioning Joshua like this, if he found it difficult to stand and look over the whole land and yet not be the one to lead the Israelites into it (Deuteronomy 34:1–4). He had come such a long way and given so many years to serving the Lord faithfully, and yet he has to stop and pass the mantle over.

SUCCESSION

There is such a challenge to us all here. We may be on the edge of seeing something great; we may long to remain part of a particular journey, in a certain area of the world; we may be steady and comfortable with leadership and familiar with all that is going on around us; and yet the Lord wants us to pass on the mantle of responsibility. There is a danger that we hold on too tight to what we want to see, and do, for the kingdom, losing sight of what God is saying and how He is guiding us.

What we love about the Lord is that He lets Moses see the land that He has promised to give to his descendants; He reminds him of His promise and reaffirms that it will happen after his death (Deuteronomy 34:4). God is faithful to Moses in effectively showing his son how far he has come. We see clearly that God is in control and not mankind – that His plans will prevail no matter what – and that we need to keep investing in future generations to continue the work after us.

Our pride can often cause us to think that things are as good as they are because we are overseeing them, and somewhere in our gut we believe that whoever takes over will never be as good or successful as we were. The story of Moses and Joshua shows us that it is never about us. The mission is about God's anointing, ministering through us, and the picture is so much bigger than what we see. Jesus is gracious enough to use us in His plans but there are plenty of others who will come after us.

Many of the best leaders we have witnessed are the ones who can let go, who can hold things lightly, who walk humbly, and who know that they are where they are because of Jesus. Those who are secure that their identity is in Christ and not in a position and as such are happy to help others coming through. Leaders for whom the overall kingdom is more important than their personal contribution. People who invest in new generations and accept that this "involves seasons of personal sacrifice to promote the spiritual and physical well-being of others to whom you are bound in an enduring relationship".[2]

When we consider that Moses and Elijah died (passing the baton on to Joshua and Elisha respectively), we cannot help but be pointed to Jesus – a leader who led knowing that it would lead Him to the cross; a leader willing to sacrifice everything for others, that they might have relationship with God. If we are to lead like Jesus, then we accept that we are children in His hands, sacrificing our wants, desires, and plans, for the sake of seeing His kingdom come in others.

Our intimacy with Jesus is absolutely key to being able to effectively pass the baton on to the generations that are rising up. We can see and know that "no prophet has risen in Israel like Moses, whom the Lord knew face to face, who did all those signs and wonders the Lord sent him to do in Egypt – to Pharaoh and to all his officials and to his whole land" (Deuteronomy 34:10–11). As one writer describes, "He possessed an intimacy of fellowship with God unknown to others, for Yahweh knew him face to face."[3] The more our mission is founded in the Lord God Almighty, and the deeper our relationship with Him goes, then the more we understand His perspective and heartbeat for those we are working with.

We believe the Lord wants to open our eyes to the future – to the generations coming after us. Moses climbs Mount Nebo from the plains of Moab to the top of Pisgah, and looks out over the whole land (Deuteronomy 34:1). Can you imagine him standing high up there, looking out as far as his eyes could see and listening to the Lord speak to him about it? How often do we pause and ask God to see a bigger picture of the land and the inhabitants around us? Do we claim it as our own land, or know that it belongs to God and wait for Him to invite us to take possession of it? Is He asking us to prophetically stand where we are so that He can open our eyes in a different way to the picture presented before us? Maybe He wants to show us someone that is in our line of vision, and speak to us about their future. Perhaps He is asking us to pray specific prayers for them so that we won't be afraid of them continuing kingdom work but aiding them in their equipping. **God may**

be asking some of us to move from where we are standing, or to lay down our leadership, or to step out of the way for the next person to lead. The question is, have we even asked Him if we should?!

It's fascinating what Moses says to Joshua – "Be strong and courageous" – and he doesn't just say it once; he speaks it over him repeatedly (Deuteronomy 31:7, 23). Moses is obviously concerned that the next leader of Israel needs to be bold in taking possession of the land. We wonder whether he privately questioned, "Surely it's not Joshua, Lord? He is not full of courage." And yet he knows himself and his weakness well enough, and the power of God enough, that He can commission the great "Son of Nun". Perhaps Moses turned his concerns into prayer for Joshua, and he spoke them into his life frequently as a way of building him up, in preparation for the next phase of his journey.

HOW CAN WE HELP?

What are those around us lacking? Do they need to be strong and courageous like Joshua? Do we need to begin to pray that over their lives? Maybe they need the double portion that Elisha was asking for? Even if they think they don't, we should still ask the Lord to give it to them.

When we think about our own children, our prayers and longing are that they would know Jesus in a deeper way than we do and have a heart to serve Him with everything in them. We are hungry that they would see more than we could ever ask or imagine, according to His power at work within them (Ephesians 3:20). We long that they might know the Lord like Moses did, "face to face", and become great agents of change. These are our children by blood, and so our heart cry makes sense. However, wouldn't it be amazing if as a church we could begin to dream more for our spiritual children and grandchildren, praying these sorts of prayers for them? What do we dream of for the next generation? What do we long to see happen in future years? What kind of legacy will we leave for them?

Joshua must have felt pretty terrified taking up the mantle from Moses – to follow a man who was "God's chosen charismatic leader in Israel, God's spokesman, God's agent"[4] must have been so challenging. Yes, he needed to be brave going into the land, but he also needed to have courage to lead the people onwards. It makes us wonder what kind of leadership we are modelling in this day and age. Is it leadership that feels too "separate" or "impossible to aspire to" – or perhaps it is too costly?

It can be very challenging and costly to be a Christian. **It is absolutely vital that we invest and build into the younger generations**, so that they are ready to carry the kingdom mantle around the world. We need to "speak the truth in love" and be authentic about what walking with Jesus really looks like. The reality is that He invites all of us to follow Him – He loves the least, the lowest, and the lost, and He can use them in incredible ways to change the world.

Elisha asks the question, "Where now is the Lord, the God of Elijah?" (2 Kings 2:14). We believe that He is waiting for a generation of Elishas that we have invested in, to go further than we ever could dream or imagine. So **let's go find our Elishas and give them all we can that they might go further than we ever could**.

YES! But how?

YOU AND GOD

Personal reflection:

- Who are the Elishas that you are investing in?
- Are there any others that God is leading you to?
- Is there a situation you are in where it might be time to "pass the baton" and trust God for your future?
- What else can you put in their hand to help them to take over?
- Are we praying for future generations, asking God to give them what they need to go further?

Looking back...

Think back about the people who have invested in you. What have they done for you? This may be people in your life, your faith or your work. How have they supported you? What opportunities have they given you? How did they do it? What was the impact on them? What was the impact on you?

GROUP ACTIVITY

1. Moses climbs Mount Nebo from the plains of Moab to the top of Pisgah and looks out over the whole land (Deuteronomy 34:1). Encourage the group to close their eyes and, in silence, imagine themselves high up a mountain or a hill, looking down at the land they know well. It may be their community, their school, workplace or church (wherever they invest their time and energy). Then pray that God would speak to them about whom

they should be investing in. Who are the Joshuas and Elishas that He wants to show to them? Perhaps there are already some that the group are investing in but He wants us to challenge or invest in them in a new way? There may be others on our landscape that God wants to draw our attention to. Quietly ask Him what He wants us to do. Wait and listen. Pray together for God to open doors with these people. Let's be part of raising up future generations!

2. Use a picture of a baton or, even better, get your hands on a baton, or something that looks like one. Pass the baton around the group, or around the leaders that are visible (if there are lots of people). Encourage those doing it/ listening to consider what they are holding tightly in their lives and ministry. What do they struggle to pass over or lay down? In what ways do they not want to pass the baton to the next person? Perhaps there is fear or a lack of trust. Read Romans 12:1–2: "Therefore, I urge you, brothers and sisters, in view of God's mercy, to offer your bodies as a living sacrifice, holy and pleasing to God – this is your true and proper worship. Do not conform to the pattern of this world, but be transformed by the renewing of your mind. Then you will be able to test and approve what God's will is – his good, pleasing and perfect will."

It may be helpful to have one of these playing in the background or sing together:

"I surrender" – Hillsong Live, from the album *Cornerstone* (2012 DVD)

"Living for your glory (Take my life let it be, everything all of me)" by Tim Hughes, from the album *Hold Nothing Back*

RECOMMENDED RESOURCE FOR MENTORING/TRAINING LEADERS:

Reverend Dr Kate Coleman is the founding director of Next Leadership. She has nearly thirty years of leadership experience in the church, charity, and voluntary sectors and is a mentor and coach to leaders. Visit her website for more information on how to be raised up and raise up other Elishas: www.nextleadership.org/about-us/#

Further reading

R. Hassall, *Growing Young Leaders: A Practical Guide to Mentoring Teens* (Oxford: BRF, 2009)
J. Lawrence, *Growing Leaders: Reflections on Leadership, Life and Jesus* (Oxford: BRF, 2004)

14
Investing in New Generations

"The greatness of a man is not in how much wealth he acquires, but in his integrity and his ability to affect those around him positively."

BOB MARLEY

In the thirteen years of his life, Jake's difficult background had taught him to fight his way through each day. His dad walked out on his mum when he was only a few weeks old, leaving her to get by on what benefits the social services were prepared to offer – and they were few. His box room on the eighteenth floor of the filthy, towering council flats may not have looked like much, but Jake called it home. When he was ten years old a local church youth worker called Alan moved onto his estate and began a lifestyle of relational evangelistic youth work. At first Jake was highly suspicious of this member of "the God squad". He couldn't understand why a middle-class man from the nice side of town would come and live there out of choice.

Jake and his friends made life as hard as possible for Alan. They spat in his face, slashed the tyres on his dilapidated Vauxhall Astra, and did anything they could think of to discredit his endeavours. Despite their best efforts there was no displacing Alan. He felt a clear calling from God to be in that place so he bravely persevered in his difficult surroundings. Even so, after the best part of three years serving on the estate Alan began to feel a little disillusioned about whether or not it was all worth it. Why would God have brought him here only for nothing to happen and for him to feel entirely hopeless? Thankfully, by God's grace, he was about to see some reward for his tireless efforts. On a cold winter night he sat with Jake on a rickety, graffiti-stained bench sharing his Thermos flask of tea. Despite the falling temperature and rising wind, the pair of them talked for over two hours, about Jesus. At the end of the conversation Alan had the privilege of witnessing Jake coming to the point of surrendering his life to the King of kings. This was more than Alan had dreamed possible. After three years of battling against the odds, here was one of the estate ringleaders giving his life to Jesus. That night, for the first time in over twenty years, Alan was so excited that he didn't get a wink of sleep.

In the weeks that followed, Jake started out on the adventure of being a Christian. As Alan discipled him he knew that he was being transformed. He was being kinder to those around him, and felt a greater sense of meaning, worth, and destiny. Jake started to see the folly of his previous ways as the chip on his shoulder became non-existent and slipped away. He also began praying, reading the Bible, and going to church. Having always assumed that church was boring, Jake was pleasantly surprised to find that he actually quite enjoyed it. However, he did find it hard that he was just about the only teenager there. After he had been going to the church every Sunday for about nine months, his minister preached on baptism and offered individuals the opportunity to be baptized (as Jesus Himself had been). Jake knew straight away that this was for him. The minute the service was over, he headed straight for the minister. Together they agreed that Jake should be baptized.

Jake went to the worst school of hard knocks in the area – an inner-city boys' comprehensive. He bravely invited his entire form group of thirty to his baptismal service. Amazingly, about twenty or so of them agreed. He told them to get to the church in good time, sit on the back rows, and "Be patient with the old people at church. They aren't used to young people and may not know how to relate to you."

When the day of the baptism finally came, people began filling up the pews. The adults arriving at the church were somewhat stunned and intimidated by the rough-looking lads sat on the back couple of rows. After all, Jake was the only young person at the church. The regular church attendees tried to conceal quite how uncomfortable they were feeling. Their efforts were in vain, as it was perfectly clear to anyone in the building that the women were terrified. The men tried to act cool, but it was obvious that their hands were firmly in their pockets clinging tightly to mobile phones, car keys, and wallets. That Sunday morning there were no people to be seen raising their arms during worship for fear of their pockets being emptied!

Eventually the time came for Jake to give his testimony: "You may have noticed something different this morning. Unlike the rest of you here I have actually invited some people to come to church that don't yet know Jesus." This comment from the plucky young lad at the front caused corporate shock throughout the congregation. The silence invoked by this seemed to last for an eternity. Alan, however, sat there with the widest possible smile across his face, feeling incredibly proud of Jake and blown away by the God who's in the business of changing lives. Eventually Jake continued: "I've told them to make a decision about Christianity based on how you treat them after the service." This time a nervous laughter swept through the congregation. These young lads at the back were not the church type. Not one member of the regular congregation had any desire to go anywhere near them.

When the baptisms were over the scenes that followed were quite remarkable. Through a mixture of guilt and obligation the adults began to gather around the young lads like a swarm of bees. These now poor, defenceless young lads each had ten to fifteen adults surrounding them and offering them more and more polystyrene cups of tea and custard cream biscuits. For one day only the church could have done with some emergency portaloos!

WHAT IT ALL MEANS

The story of Jake is a wonderful one. Here is a young man who truly lives out what it means to be a Christian. He is part of the local Christian community, yet also inhabits the outside world (Matthew 5:13–16). He enjoys worshipping at church but is also keen to spread the gospel message (Romans 1:15). He loves his Christian family yet is unafraid to challenge them (1 Corinthians 14:36). We dream of a whole church that is one day full of Jake-type characters of all ages, shapes, and sizes. We as a church need to raise our game. At the moment we simply aren't cutting it in terms of evangelism. We need to focus our efforts and reach out to the world in love (Matthew 19:19).

Moving the furniture, redesigning the programme, and entertaining the children are all good and right, but not in place of reaching our world. Young people are vitally important to the church's future. If we want to change the world then our efforts need to be largely refocused on the young. After all, a recent research study by the Evangelical Alliance showed that 86 per cent of those who become Christians in the UK do so under the age of twenty-five.[1] This should radically affect how a church operates. We've tested the statistic in many churches by asking people to put their hands up if they came to Jesus under the age of twenty-five. Nearly every hand goes up! Therefore, if we want to have a vibrant, growing church then we need to invest in the young. We wonder whether or not your church invests 86 per cent of its resources for home mission into young people, as this would seem the logical correlation in terms of missionary activity!

For the majority of young people today, you never know what's waiting just around the corner. The difficult and disengaging teenagers of today could, with the right investment, go on to be tomorrow's Christian heroes. It's interesting to look through the pages of church history and see the ages at which many of our leaders came to faith: Charles Spurgeon (15), George Whitefield (16), William Booth (15), C. T. Studd (16), James Hudson Taylor (15), D. L. Moody (18), Amy Carmichael (15), and Billy Graham (17).[2] We're deeply excited at the prospect of some of these Christians being reached and raised up today. However, if this is to happen then significant change is required. The game needs changing.

FURTHER INVESTMENT?

In research for his first book, *Disappointed with Jesus?*, Gavin surveyed two hundred young people about the type of youth leaders they would like. **Over 85 per cent primarily wanted a parent/grandparent figure**.[3] This destroys one commonly held theory that the best people to do youth ministry are the older brother/sister type. Often young people have siblings and older friends, but what they are really lacking is a parent/grandparent type. It is into this sociological situation that a church full of parent and grandparent figures has an amazing missionary opportunity to a hurting generation of young people.

We love the potential within the church for the generations to serve one another. When you combine the enthusiasm of youth with the wisdom of age you have an amazing combination. We can think of many people who can become worn down and cynical through their experiences of church; yet, when they see the vibrancy and enthusiasm of a young Christian, it rubs off on them and the cynicism quickly falls away. Equally, there are myriad younger Christians who benefit hugely from the help of those more mature in the faith. A church of all ages, shapes, and sizes is a rich body that can make a radical difference – to themselves first, then to their community, their culture, and their world. The church just has to take the needs of the young seriously.

Most of us who come to faith do so as young people, and it must be fundamental to any future growth and development of the church for us to reach out in love to a new generation. In a world where young people are more insecure than ever, we need the church to support and offer unqualified acceptance and love. Many people often say young people are worse today but this is simply not true. In the eighth century BC the Greek poet Hesiod said, "I see no hope for the future of our people if they are dependent on the frivolous youth of today, for certainly all youth are reckless beyond words… **When I was young, we were taught to be discreet and respectful of elders, but the present youth are exceedingly wise, disrespectful and impatient of restraint.**" Young people are not worse today. They have always been our greatest hope and yet our biggest challenge. However, Britain is arguably more "broken" than ever before. But who broke Britain? Not the young people. We need to support teenagers today in the challenging landscape they grow up in.

Equally, if the church still wants to be in healthy existence in the West in thirty years' time, then it must reach a new and younger crowd. It is frightening to witness an ageing church. The annual conferences are filled with the same people getting older every year. The church needs a new input of youth. Young people have the potential to take more risks. They have fewer commitments and are therefore able to try things that most of us wouldn't dare. The church desperately needs the vibrant cutting edge that a massive intravenous injection of younger people would produce. The results could be gloriously dangerous – but that is why our God has so often chosen those younger in Jesus to drive his people forward.

The Bible is littered with examples of old and young working together for the good of the kingdom. In Exodus 18, our key character in this book, Moses, needs some help. Even though he has faced the Lord at the burning bush (Exodus 3), and seen the Red Sea split before his eyes (Exodus 14), Moses needs some advice from someone who has been around a little longer. Into this situation steps his father-in-law, Jethro. He is upset to see that Moses is sitting alone as judge over all the people. Therefore, he tells him to share the load. It is simply too much for Moses to hope to do on his own, and Jethro's wisdom and experience make it easier for him to observe this in his son-in-law. Here is a man who has done amazing things, will soon receive the Ten Commandments from the top of Mount Sinai (Exodus 20), and yet even he needed a little gentle steering from an older head.

For all the many great instances within the Bible of multi-generational investment, Jesus has to be the ultimate example of how it should be done. Jesus in his early thirties took on twelve younger men aged between their mid-teens and early twenties. He lived amongst them, developed them, sought out their opinions, and gave them opportunities to do things even though He could do them better Himself. He encouraged them to take risks (Matthew 14), used their efforts to great effect (John 6), and forgave the ultimate denial (John 21). When Jesus found, and called, His twelve disciples, what He really did was form the first youth group. Here was an older person bothering to invest in the up and coming when many others would have seen it as risky or too much like hard work. We may feel that we don't have enough time to invest in teenagers, yet Jesus' three-year earthly ministry was primarily spent investing in younger people. Surely if Jesus made such a priority of passing on to others what He had to offer, then we should find the time to do the same? Jesus gives us a wonderful example of what it means to develop a new generation.

From whatever angle you come at it, young people need older people to invest in them. Whoever you are, whatever you're like, wherever you live, **we must be giving support to those younger than ourselves**. More than twenty-five years ago an adventurous challenge was made in a book to evangelical Christians in Britain. It was claimed that churches were emptying, worship was often dull and turgid, and new excitement was needed. An older leader – Revd Gilbert Kirby, who was respected by many of his generation – put his neck on the line and endorsed the challenge of a younger man even though he realized that many would mock him for doing so. But the author of the book was Gavin's dad, and Gilbert Kirby his grandpa. The older man's support gave the younger man courage. The same remains true today.

There is a much-celebrated secular youth work saying: "It takes one significant adult to change a young person's worldview, morality, and lifestyle forever." This is an incredible reality. By just one adult bothering to invest in a young person's life we can help that young person realize what really matters. Just one adult can help a young person make informed decisions on things, view the world in a new way, and honour themselves and those around them through their behaviour.

Now as a church we are not just here to make bad people good; we are really here to help dead people live, and our churches throughout the UK are full of significant adults. Just think how many younger people would be reached and changed if these adults were mobilized – action that led to not just bad people being made good but dead people living forever! It is the responsibility of the current adult population to provide a positive example and to mentor the next generation. When the then Prime Minister Tony Blair decided that every young person in Britain needed to have a mentor of some sort it was as if he himself had come up with the idea of mentoring new leadership. Not so – the Bible reveals that people have been practising it for thousands of years. We need a generation of adults who invest in young people, wanting them to be all they can be.

HELPING NEW GENERATIONS THRIVE

One of the key points of mentoring is helping the younger person to avoid many of the mistakes made previously, thus enabling them to be more fully equipped for life. We must want the next generation to be better than us. Why? So that they can see things happening for the kingdom of God that right now seem a distant possibility.

We know too many older folk who are happy to mentor younger people until they seem to be way in advance of them; pastors who will only let a younger person share their pulpit until that individual portrays a stronger flair, or anointing, for preaching than them. Then, all of a sudden, the opportunities disappear. For the sake of God and His kingdom we must get rid of this mentality and begin to work together. We need to encourage a new generation with a greater portion of the Spirit, as this might lead to us finally seeing a growth and renewal in the church like we have not seen since the Welsh Revival of more than a hundred years ago. The older generations need to be secure enough to want the new to have a double portion, or ten times the portion, of the Spirit that they have. After all, we are essentially in a family business. It is not about my ministry and me, but instead it must be about God and His kingdom.

Gavin was very blessed when he served at Youth for Christ to have intergenerational investment modelled to him by his then boss, Roy Crowne. Roy gave him a chance on the leadership team of YFC when, at just twenty-three, Gavin was far younger than most. Few would have taken the risk! He took on someone with evangelical baggage when many others would have preferred him to be out of the way. He did not just leave Gavin to get on with it; he was always there investing, using his experience to save him from costly mistakes – and opening doors for him, which as a younger man he could not have done alone.

Gavin will always be grateful to Roy for the trust that he placed in him, and the support he gave him. Moreover, what Roy did for Gavin has meant that whatever he goes on to do with his life, and wherever that may be, he will always be looking for ways to invest in, and help to raise up, the next generation. For what we model now will be repeated. If we invest in others, then perhaps they may do the same with those that come after them. Of course, if we reject new generations, we need not be surprised if they too, one day, reject us. What grieves us is to see so many of our peers, and the generations below us, not being given similar support. We have been given the chance to flourish, while many of our peers have had the opposite experience. We believe it is imperative that the church of Jesus Christ begins to prepare for the future, instead of being content to reminisce about the past.

Personally, and professionally, it is the responsibility of the church to help younger people become all that they can be for tomorrow, not just satisfied to live in the good of yesterday. We mustn't fall into the trap of believing that it is too soon for some of today's young people. We regularly hear that we should just give them a few years to grow up or become old enough to make a difference. Yet Jeremiah was only a boy, David was the youngest of Jesse's sons, and as we've said, the disciples were a youth group. We need to help these people now. It's not too soon. Let's engage with and assist a new generation. Let's support them where perhaps we weren't supported, give them opportunities where we were denied them, and save young people from making the same mistakes we made.

As you read this we wonder whether or not you are personally committed – practically, prayerfully, and financially – in nurturing younger people? Are you passing on what you have learned? Are you dreaming with the next generation about what could be? Are you secure enough to want them to have a double portion of anything you've got? It doesn't need to be that difficult. You could have a cup of coffee with a few younger people every couple of weeks to encourage them. You could try to talk to some of those on the outside whom no one loves. You could give the church youth leader a financial gift to help with the young. Maybe you could just begin to assume that young people aren't always bad and could really benefit from your help. If you are not currently making things different for a new generation then please begin to invest, as they desperately need your help. You have so much wisdom, experience, and life to share.

After all, it only takes one significant adult…

YES! But how?

YOU AND GOD

Pastor Rick Warren from Saddleback Church in the USA gives us some helpful advice for praying for others. Why not use this as a tool for praying for those that you are investing in:

In Philippians 1:9–11, Paul spells out exactly what he's praying for people:

> *"And this is my prayer: that your love may abound more and more in knowledge and depth of insight, so that you may be able to discern what is best and be pure and blameless until the day of Christ, filled with the fruit of righteousness that comes through Jesus Christ – to the glory and praise of God."*

These verses give you four things you can pray for people today:

- "Abound in love…" Pray that they will grow in love.
- "Discern what is best…" Pray that they make wise choices.
- "Be pure and blameless…" Pray that they will do the right thing.
- "Filled with the fruit of righteousness…" Pray that they will live for God's glory.

For the extended version see:
http://rickwarren.org/devotional/english/pray-for-others_508

Others...

Think of the children and young people you have contact with – they may be your children, godchildren, nieces, nephews, grandchildren, friends' children, young people at your church or those whom you work with. Make a list of ways you could encourage them, celebrate their gifts or give them opportunities to shine. Make a plan to implement those ideas within the next month.

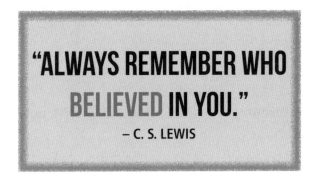

"ALWAYS REMEMBER WHO BELIEVED IN YOU."
– C. S. LEWIS

GROUP ACTIVITY

1. Consider the following:

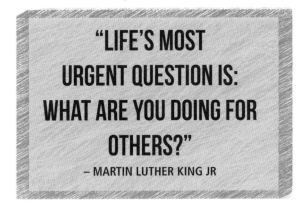

"LIFE'S MOST URGENT QUESTION IS: WHAT ARE YOU DOING FOR OTHERS?"
– MARTIN LUTHER KING JR

Have a chat as a group or with the person next to you about the different things that you do for others. How can you encourage and pray for one another over these areas? Remember it only takes one significant adult!

2. Why not take a few minutes to consider who has invested in you. Corporately thank Jesus for bringing them into your lives and for taking time to care. Think for another few minutes about what they did to invest in you. Was it financial, did they take time to listen, encourage, challenge, etc.? Which area did you find the most helpful? Is there a way that God is asking you to pass that on to others in your life? Share with one other person what you are committing to do.

Some resource websites for working with new generations:

Care for the Family: www.careforthefamily.org.uk/shop/faith-resources/getting-your-kids-through-church-dvd-pack
Scripture Union: www.scriptureunion.org.uk/LightLive
Urban Saints: www.energize.uk.net/
Youth for Christ: www.yfc.co.uk/resources

Further reading

G. Calver, *Disappointed with Jesus?* (Oxford: Monarch Books, 2010)
G. Calver, S. Whiting, *Lazy, Anti-Social & Selfish?* (Oxford: Monarch Books, 2009)
R. Gardner, *Beloved* (Nottingham: IVP, 2015)
R. Parsons, *Getting Your Kids Through Church Without Them Ending Up Hating God* (Oxford: Monarch Books, 2011)
L. Sweet, *I Am a Follower* (Nashville: Thomas Nelson Publishing, 2012)

15
The Best is Yet to Come

"Hope is being able to see that there is light despite all of the darkness."

DESMOND TUTU

ike many men of his age, Gavin finds that when he's asked what his favourite film is there is a choice of three: the original *Rocky*, *Jaws* or *The Shawshank Redemption*. In the end he predictably plumps for *Shawshank*. It's an incredible movie that, despite poor financial takings in the cinemas when first released, has gone on to be considered one of the greatest of all time. In this film the lead character, Andy Dufresne (excellently played by Tim Robbins), is locked up in prison for killing his wife and the guy she was having an affair with, even though he is entirely innocent of both crimes. Once inside and serving his sentence, he receives two weeks in solitary confinement for playing a Mozart record over the loudspeaker system that runs throughout the prison.

On completion of his stint in solitary, he is asked by his friend Red (played spectacularly by Morgan Freeman) whether it had been worth spending all that time on his own just to have heard that one short piece of Mozart. Andy says one thing that is arresting. He declares that he needs not to forget. Forget what? That the one thing the prison guards cannot control or take away is the hope inside each prisoner. The music gave him hope and reminded him of the deeper things in his life that no grey walls could cage.

We as a church need to cling on to hope. However bleak or challenging things might seem, we need to believe. We must hope for our prodigals, hope for our communities, hope for breakthrough, hope for the game to change. We must never let this hope stop. We need to fan it into flame and keep believing. Let's keep hoping.

A hope that this nation could be transformed forever. Not in a superficial or short-term way, but forever! Gavin remembers as a seventeen-year-old being interested in a General Election for the first time. He was disappointed to be just a year shy of qualifying to vote but remembers staying up until the early hours as the Tony Blair-inspired "New Labour" revolution grew great pace with a massive landslide victory. This took place with coffee cups in hand, and a new type of politician was born, whilst playing out to the music of D:Ream declaring that "Things can only get better." Doubtless it did their record sales no harm, and for a while it seemed like things would change forever but, in truth, when it comes to societal change we as the church must want more. We don't want to just change the language, redecorate the landscape, and give birth to soundbites. We need complete cultural transformation for Christ.

Russell Brand has made the headlines for many different things in recent times, and whether you agree with him on many issues or not, he's certainly on a journey. He speaks into culture profoundly, though perhaps at times overestimates a little how much of the new generation he actually represents. Nonetheless he speaks often about the fact that he believes "it's time for a spiritual revolution". He's shared this message over many different mediums and we find ourselves agreeing with him on this point. We don't want things to get a bit better; we want them to change completely. We look at so much hopelessness around, so many struggles, and know that the only real answer is Christ. Having spent fourteen years serving at Youth for Christ, it became evident to us that young people are desperately seeking something greater and that whatever else they may try, in the end the only thing that will satisfy is God. The French mathematician and Christian philosopher Blaise Pascal was right when he wrote about a vacuum within each one of us that cannot be filled by anything but Jesus. So we really do need a Jesus revolution – an entire overhaul of the current culture and a positioning of Christ as King.

The Greek philosopher Aristotle said that **"hope is a waking dream".** We need to keep holding to that hope, pursuing it and growing it – hope that this Jesus actually is earth shattering, loving, and the provider of freedom. A hope that there is something greater than rituals and committees; that the church is about leaving the building and changing our communities. Fears may try to capture, but the hope cannot be caged. Like Andy Dufresne, let's not quit hoping that there is something greater. If hope is allowed to die, then what is left?

FAITH FOR CHANGE

We have real reason to believe things can change. **Throughout history every so often a bunch of people get hold of a God-given passion and change their environment.** It takes a worldview described in Hebrews 11:1, where it says that "faith is confidence in what we hope for and assurance about what we do not see". We need to have confidence in what we want to see change and yet be certain that God is alongside us. We take huge comfort from Jesus' words in John 14:12, where He says, "Very truly I tell you, whoever believes in me will do the works I have been doing, and they will do even greater things than these, because I am going to the Father." When we look at what Jesus did in His earthly ministry the idea that we might ever see greater things taking place is staggering.

Canadian author Malcolm Gladwell wrote a famous book, *The Tipping Point*, looking at what it takes to change a culture. He describes it like this:

> *The tipping point is that magic moment when an idea, trend, or social behaviour crosses a threshold, tips, and spreads like wildfire. Just as a single sick person can start an epidemic of the flu, so too can a small but precisely targeted push cause a fashion trend, the popularity of a new product, or a drop in the crime rate.*[1]

We as the church could be so active in our land that we create a tipping point at which the church becomes unstoppable in her mission!

As well as action it also takes faith. Jesus says in Matthew 17:20, "Truly I tell you, if you have faith as small as a mustard seed, you can say to this mountain, 'Move from here to there,' and it will move. Nothing will be impossible for you." We need to be a people of faith prepared to live out what we believe and share with those around us. We really could see some incredible things happen, and yet we wonder sometimes whether we are too scared, disengaged or self-absorbed. We need to make our lives count, listen to the voice of God over the crowd, and make an impact through our lives in this land.

Gavin had been a Christian for about six months when, aged eighteen, he headed out to church one Sunday night. He was still a bit stiff from the day's football match and in truth was not as excited about the service ahead of him as he sometimes was. He was going to go, do his duty, and then get home as quickly as he could. He sat uncomfortably in the pew and listened for all of the first thirty seconds of the sermon before tuning out totally. Once the preacher man had finished, his mind wandered as he sat there deciding between a trip to the pub to see the boys or going straight home. Decision made, he prepared to leave for the pub, and as he got up the band launched into a final song. Suddenly he felt rude leaving so stayed to finish the song. The band belted out the then well-known Delirious song "History Maker". As they sang Gavin was compelled to fall to his knees. Head in his hands, he had a powerful encounter with the Lord. He felt God challenging him directly to give his life to trying to make a difference in this land. In his soul Gavin sensed that he and the Lord would go on many great adventures and that he simply needed to join in. Having fully surrendered his life to Jesus those few months earlier, Gavin made a second major promise. He declared that he would go "wherever, whenever, and into whatever for God". It was a big step.

In Matthew 16:24–26 Jesus says, "Whoever wants to be my disciple must deny themselves and take up their cross and follow me. For whoever wants to save their life will lose it, but whoever loses their life for me will find it. What good will it be for someone to gain the whole world, yet forfeit their soul?" That night in church it felt like Gavin was laying his whole life on an altar before God and saying, "It's yours." In return he felt the Lord saying He wanted to use him in some way to make history for Him.

Fast-forward eighteen years or so and Gavin was sat in our lounge having a coffee with a friend. "What is it that drives you?" his friend asked. "I want to change the world. Not for me; I want to change the world for Jesus or die trying," Gavin replied. Initially his friend seemed shocked but eventually a wry smile came across his face. "That's great," he said. "I wish a few more people felt like that." We do too! We don't want to be people living in a dream, but we do believe that we as the people of God are called to change the world. We're compelled to be visionary, painting and living out a different existence than the rest. We are to influence, not be influenced, and bring about change. Many of our contemporaries also sang about being "history makers" a couple of decades ago, but over the years that have passed since so many have grown tired, cynical, dropped away or just given up. Under the authority of Jesus and in His name we can change the world, and we want to be part of a radical remnant of Christians who truly choose to be game changers.

This land has been in Christian decline for too long. Perhaps you could call it perennial decline, but it's not terminal! The stats don't look great, the picture isn't perfect, but God has not given up on the UK church. However, we need to be prepared to be changed and to be countercultural in order to see our nation impacted. **We need to stop being people of entitlement seeking to have all our wants and needs met and transition into people consumed by the Living God and prepared to be sold out for Him whatever the price tag.**

If you read through church history you'll see it's been far worse than this and the Lord has done amazing things here in the past. So why not now too?! We truly believe that in our lifetime we will see an incredible revival in the UK. Things have to turn around, hope hasn't died, and we will see change. For us the only option other than seeing this incredible move of God would be to die believing it's coming the next day! We are choosing to be people of hope, to say to the Lord that all we are is His, to pray fervently for change and to do all we can to encourage and enthuse others that here in Britain when it comes to Christianity we have a greater future than we've had a past. In short, the best is yet to come!

IT'S NOT A FAIRY TALE

It won't always be easy. Being a hopeful person will sometimes be hard, and in the light of the challenge we choose to remain hopeful. We don't deny the struggles, we aren't flippant about suffering, and we don't pretend to live in some fairy tale where everyone lives happily ever after. No – we face up to our reality and bring hope into what can often seem a barren land. We see light where others see darkness. We see opportunity where some might see desolation. We choose to look upwards to Him and not in front of us at the mess and distractions.

At no point did this Christianity thing claim to be an easy ride. James 1:2–3 stresses quite the opposite: "Consider it pure joy, my brothers and sisters, whenever you face trials of many kinds, because you know that the testing of your faith develops perseverance." The Christian life is tough but it's well worth it. In the struggles and the trials we keep hoping. We aren't stopped, we push on, and we remain those who are trying to do something different with our lives and in the world.

We are not alone in needing to remain hopeful with a kingdom perspective even when the life we're living is challenging. In his commentary on James, David Field points us towards the example of Jesus: He spent most of His ministry struggling or under pressure. He had nowhere He could truly call home, He wept by his friend's tomb (John 11); He was constantly being watched and accused of breaking Pharisaical laws (Matthew 12); He felt profound compassion for His people and their needs (Matthew 9:36); He sweated with mental agony in the garden of Gethsemane (Matthew 26), and died in torment on the cross (Matthew 27). Significantly, He also warned His followers that they would not escape the stresses and strains that He himself had to face (Matthew 5).[2] Funny that most of us claim to want to be Christ-like but would hate to ever have to walk the paths He did!

We need to realize that it won't always be a nice, comfortable existence. In truth, the more honest we are about some of the struggles, the better. The harder life is for us the greater God needs to be to help us get through. We realize how amazing He is when we see what else is around. We also find in the struggle that we're in total agreement with the words of John Newton (whom we encountered earlier in this book too) in the incredible film with the same title of the famous hymn he wrote, *Amazing Grace*: **"Although my memory's fading, I remember two things very clearly. I'm a great sinner and Christ is a great Saviour."**[3] We think that sometimes we can be arrogant enough to forget our need of a Saviour but we must remember what He's done for us and how much we need Him.

Things will go wrong in life. To quote a Christian cliché: "We live in a fallen world." For us, though, the question is not "Why does God allow suffering?" or "Where is God when we're struggling?" but "Are you walking closely with Him through the struggle?" After all, a relationship that just finishes when it gets hard is not worth a great deal. Relationship with commitment means so much, but without our commitment, what is a Christian life worth? We need to stick with Jesus, persevere, and keep hoping. Mary Stevenson puts it superbly in the wonderful old "Footprints" poem: "I love you and would never, never leave you. During your times of trial and suffering when you see only one set of footprints… It was then that I carried you."

This Christian life is not to be done by halves. When you surrender your life to Jesus you give Him everything – where you live, who you do or don't marry, what you do, how you love, your time, devotion and so on. All of your life is His. You don't hold something back for yourself. It won't always be easy, but the wonderful news is that we'll never be alone! He is with us.

HOPE FOR TOMORROW

So life won't be perfect but our hope needs to endure. In the face of this reality one line from the famous hymn "Great is thy faithfulness" comes to mind. What we need as we build a better future is "Strength for today and bright hope for tomorrow".[4] Strength to see above our reality and imagine what could be in our family, workplace, sports team, community, church, and nation. Strength to keep going in the face of challenge, and strength to keep pursuing Christ and His agenda. This then needs to marry a bright hope for tomorrow. Hope that things will be different, hope that can't be extinguished, and hope that inspires us to change things. We've talked a lot about hope in this chapter and in truth we don't find it as hard to muster as some. Therefore, if as you're reading you are wanting to be hopeful and yet not knowing where to start, perhaps you might like to begin by praying "A Prayer of Hope"…

Heavenly Father,

I am your humble servant; I come before you today in need of hope. There are times when I feel helpless; there are times when I feel weak. I pray for hope. I need hope for a better future. I need hope for a better life. I need hope for love and kindness.

Some say that the sky is at its darkest just before the light. I pray that this is true, for all seems dark. I need your light, Lord, in every way.

I pray to be filled with your light from head to toe. To bask in your glory. To know that all is right in the world, as you have planned, and as you want it to be.

Help me to walk in your light, and live my life in faith and glory.

In your name I pray,

Amen.[5]

YES! But how?

YOU AND GOD

We are people of hope

Hope – write a list of the things that give you hope. Write some on Post-it notes and stick them around your house in places that will encourage you. Cling to hope whatever lies in front of you!

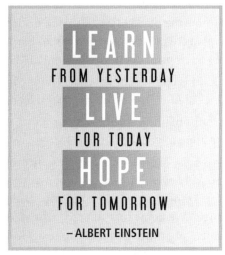

LEARN FROM YESTERDAY
LIVE FOR TODAY
HOPE FOR TOMORROW

– ALBERT EINSTEIN

Read this verse of Scripture over yourself as a prayer today, asking God to cause His truth to permeate your life: "And so, Lord, where do I put my hope? My only hope is in you" (Psalm 39:7, NLT).

GROUP ACTIVITY

1. Gather any verses you can around the theme of hope. Perhaps use the three here to get you started. You could print lots of them and scatter them on the floor, then ask a

few people to come and pray, pick one up, and go and give it to someone else. It may be someone they know, it may not; it doesn't matter. God can use the verses no matter what. Invite anyone who wants to to come and pick one up, pray, and give it to someone they feel led to give it to. You may want to play music in the background. Pray over the verses beforehand and pray over the group as they receive and read them. Don't worry if not everyone has one; the idea is that some people are really needing to know hope and have faith.

- "For I know the plans I have for you," declares the Lord, "plans to prosper you and not to harm you, plans to give you hope and a future" (Jeremiah 29:11).

- "Now faith is confidence in what we hope for and assurance about what we do not see" (Hebrews 11:1).

- "May your unfailing love be with us, Lord, even as we put our hope in you" (Psalm 33:22).

2. James 1:2–3 says, "Consider it pure joy, my brothers and sisters, whenever you face trials of many kinds, because you know that the testing of your faith develops perseverance." We know that so many Christians are facing challenging times and their hope in God must be tough, whether that is at home or abroad. Why not pray again for the worldwide church, that they might experience the joy that James is referring to. Pray that Christ would be so real in their suffering. Hold hands or put arms over the shoulders of those on your left and right, praying that Christ's hope would fill you all, equipping you to be game changers in this world, Amen.

Final Thought

> *"Parents can only give good advice or put them on the right paths, but the final forming of a person's character lies in their own hands."*
>
> ANNE FRANK

When we began writing this book, looking at the story of Moses and considering the journey that he took with the Lord, we had no idea that some of our own personal life would closely mirror this over the months ahead. It seems that whenever you write a talk and deliver a half decent sermon, you have to live the words both before, and after, you deliver them. There is a desperate need, in this day, to live authentic lives – to not just preach the Word of God but live it out in the everyday too. *Game Changers* has followed a similar vein – together we know that the words on the page have come alive in our own experiences over the last year. We have known what it is to *Encounter* Jesus in a new and compelling way. Off the back of this we have been *Enlisted* once more to join in with what the Father is doing in the nation, and have joined with others to see His kingdom come so that *Everyone* has the opportunity to be involved. We have begun to experience another level of *Equipping* through trying to listen to His voice over the world, and have sought to continue to *Empower* others to continue what the Lord is doing. None of this has been in any way easy, but it's been incredible to see and live the challenge of what we were writing in the life we were living, before the ink on the pages was even dry!

As we began delving into the story of Moses at the burning bush we realized that **he was a man who was curious and yet fearful and insecure**. He had so many questions for God and could not go any further without knowing Aaron was alongside him. About a third of the way through writing this book we went for interviews on the same day – Gavin for Director of Mission at the Evangelical Alliance and Anne for Ordination within the Baptist Union. We had no definitive idea at that stage of God's overarching plan or why these events were happening at exactly the same point! As we pushed into an encounter with God, trying to clarify what He was saying, we had questions – so many that at times it almost felt impossible for both of us to walk forward in what had clearly been birthed out of an encounter with Jesus by the power of His Holy Spirit.

Anne journeyed Moses' questions as if they were her own: "But who am I, Lord? Please send someone else!" And yet God said yes, keep walking. If you find yourself questioning an encounter with Jesus, you are not alone. If He has led you to that point, He will never leave you or forsake you. His Kingdom will come and His will will be done; we just have to say, "Yes, Lord." This can be difficult, as it has been for us, and sometimes is as simple as saying, "Lord, I will go with you and therefore am prepared to put one foot in front of the other and go where you are going, even if it's a diversion from the plans I had for my own life." For Gavin the questions were different: "Is it really time to leave YFC? Are you sure it's the Evangelical Alliance next, Lord?" With space created to encounter God, the answers to the questions came through. As a result we have been prepared to step out in faith for, and with, Him.

When we enlist as the followers of God and accept His invitation to follow Him, He is not in the business of ticking human boxes but of looking for lives of surrender. The tasks for Moses were not easy – approach your brother, whom you grew up with, take him on, and ask him to let your people go! Face Pharaoh – the human power, authority, riches, the throne – and ask him to release everyone serving him, and know that you can trust me! Wow, what a huge decision for Moses to go through with it. Yes, he was living in a foreign land, but he was settled with a wife and a son, with safety and security, looking after his father-in-law's flock, and he is called to leave it all behind.

When the Lord calls us to be His disciples, it is not easy and straightforward. As things began to change in our lives following acceptance into the BU and EA, we thought that we could easily stay in Birmingham so that Anne could finish Baptist training and Gavin could commute to the Evangelical Alliance. God had given us a great church family and friends, a lovely home near good schools, a comfortable and contented environment from which to launch out and be brave for Jesus, and pretty much all we could ask for! If this was from Him, how could He be wanting us to move? We had a fight on our hands for a while, until we realized something vital from the Lord. Praying one morning, Anne felt a reprimand: "Since when was this all about you and what you want? Who comes first?" She muttered under her shallow breath, "You, Lord."

"Then who?" she felt Him say. Anne's attention was drawn to her family and in particular Gavin. She began to think about Christ's love a bit more and the call to love others. She and her ministry were not more important than Christ and His kingdom, nor was it more important than her marriage. "I would die for Gavin," she found herself saying. "Yes, and I want you to die to yourself too," she felt the Lord imprint on her mind.

When we enlist as followers of Jesus, it isn't just about God blessing us, but about how we can bless Him too. It isn't about taking and getting, but about giving and laying down our agendas. We moved from a place of fighting, to a place of peace in surrender, with a greater trust in the Author of Life. When we sign up we don't set our own terms and conditions; we simply say, "Alright Lord, we're up for this adventure with you and trust you enough to come along even though we may feel insecure and on edge." When you read this, our prayer is that as you encounter Jesus and follow Him, that you are able to give it all to Him and know that He has an incredible journey ahead.

God did not leave Moses alone. He did not expect him to embark on the mission in solitude. He provided for him in every place that he found himself, and they were exactly the right people at the right time. He gave him family in Zipporah and Gershom, when he was grieving the loss of one, and He gave him strong Israelite companions like Aaron, Joshua, and Hur, when he had to be strong in the face of adversity.

Over the past year we have noticed a new circle of people coming around us. They are, in the main, new relationships, although some have always been there but are coming more into the fore. The more we look, the more clearly we see that God is positioning key relationships in our lives for this next season of ministry. Leaving Birmingham after fourteen years is indeed challenging, but the fear melts away a little as we look at the people in our life. For the time we've been in the Midlands the Lord has provided amazing folks, and as we step out again there will be the right co-workers, helpers, and friends once more.

God never lets us down. He always makes a way where there seems to be no way, and He will always provide a way to stand up no matter what is happening, with people who can pray, support, and love us at just the right time. The great thing is too that we are part of a church family that goes beyond nationality, let alone region, within the same nation! There are brothers and sisters in every community.

The story of the spies in Numbers teaches us such a challenging lesson about listening to the voice of the Lord even if it's manifested only in the few, rather than the majority. We know that our perspective about moving house was so selfish, and our own wants, needs, and desires so often cloud out what God might be trying to say to us. He so desperately longs to equip us to be game changers in His world, but how open are we to let Him? He will equip us with all we need. We are standing on this promise in our own lives too.

In all we do, we need to be looking for those who will come after us. Joshua was waiting in the wings, afraid and yet still the person for the job. Are we asking the Lord to raise up others to come after us? Life is short and our individual effectiveness is limited, but Jesus kept on modelling the way, the truth, and the life to His disciples. **It is never a competition between generations but instead a collaboration with one generation doing all they can to help the next go further, dream bigger, and change more than they could have**.

As we continue to transition into a new chapter of life and ministry, we hope and pray that we can keep taking others with us on the journey, demonstrating lives that are sold out for Christ, and longing to see Christ's kingdom advancing more across our nation. May our ceiling be the floor for the next generation.

We accepted the privilege of writing this book when our life looked very settled. Gavin had been serving at YFC for nearly fourteen years, Anne was serving in our local church, the kids were happy at school, we had loads of friends around us and were in a fairly comfortable stage of life. During the course of writing it our personal "game" has totally changed. Anne has got ordained, Gavin has left YFC to join the Evangelical Alliance, and we are finishing off this book from our new home in north-west London. The next stage of our adventure has begun.

All of this has been born out of a simple way of living with open hands to God, saying that we will do whatever He wants in order to try to play our own part in transforming the landscape of the UK for Christ. We know He will continue to encounter us and we are committed to making space for this. We are fully away that we need to step up and enlist to be part of it all. We are going with others and want to see everyone involved. We know He'll equip us, and we are desperate for our children's generation to be empowered and go beyond anything we will ever see.

We stand before Him with open hands, longing to be part of a church that changes the landscape of this nation, crying out to the Saviour of the world to do something incredible in this land and to allow us to be involved. Wherever, whatever, and whenever.

Will you join us?

Notes

Introduction

1. www.techopedia.com/definition/23371/digital-revolution
2. L. Sweet, *Viral* (Colorado Springs: Waterbrook Press, 2012) p.173
3. *Premier Christianity*, London, June 2015
4. F. Skinner, *Frank Skinner* (London: Arrow Books, 2001) p.96
5. *The Independent,* 31 January 2015
6. R. Brand, *Revolution* (London: Century Publishing, 2014) p.32
7. A. Motyer, *The Message of Exodus* (Nottingham: Inter-Varsity Press, 2005) p.55
8. D. Bonhoeffer, *The Cost of Discipleship* (London: SCM Press Ltd, 1959) p.104
9. A. Hirsch, *The Forgotten Ways: Reactivating the Missional Church* (Grand Rapids: Brazos, 2007) p.238
10. J. Wallis, "'I Have a Complaint' – No – 'I Have a Dream'", www.huffingtonpost.com, 30 August 2013
11. M. Macdonald, *Set Me on Fire* (Oxford: Monarch Books, 2015) p.7

Chapter 1

1. P. Moore, *Straight to the Heart of Moses* (Oxford: Monarch Books, 2011) p.27
2. J. P. Hyatt, *Exodus* (London: Marshall, Morgan & Scott Ltd., 1971) p.72
3. A. Cole, *Exodus* (Leicester: Inter-Varsity Press, 1979) p.66
4. D. Randall, article entitled "Lack of time! Perception or reality" on www.witi.com
5. D. Bannatyne, *Anyone Can Do It*, abbreviated from an article at www.zimeye.com
6. S. R. Covey, *The 7 Habits of Highly Effective People* (London: Simon & Schuster, 2004) p. 151

Chapter 2

1. P. Moore, *Straight to the Heart of Moses* (Oxford: Monarch Books, 2011) p.30
2. E. Peterson, *Eat this Book* (London: Hodder & Stoughton, 2006) p.65
3. S. Lloyd-Jones, *The Jesus Storybook Bible* (Nashville: Thomas Nelson Publishing, 2007) pp.348–349
4. C. Rogers, *Immeasurably More* (Oxford: Monarch Books, 2014) p.153
5. A. Motyer, *The Message of Exodus* (Nottingham: Inter-Varsity Press, 2005) p.60
6. J. Newton (1725–1807), "Amazing Grace"

Chapter 3

1. www.statisticbrain.com/attention-span-statistics/
2. S. Young, *Jesus Calling* (Nashville: Thomas Nelson Inc., 2007) p.117
3. S. Lambert, *A Book of Sparks* (Watford: Instant Apostle, 2012) p.91
4. B. Hybels, *Too Busy Not to Pray* (Nottingham: Inter-Varsity Press, 2011) p.13
5. K. Kandiah, *Route 66* (Oxford: Monarch Books, 2011) p.34
6. www.biblesociety.org.uk/about-bible-society/our-work/lectio-divina/

7. B. Hybels, *Too Busy Not to Pray* (Nottingham: Inter-Varsity Press, 2011) p.14

8. For further information and resources visit: www.biblesociety.org.uk/about-bible-society/our-work/lectio-divina/

9. M. Breen, *Building a Discipling Culture* (Pawleys Island: 3DM Publishing, 2014)
Note: Mike Breen headings with prayers adapted by the writers of this book

Chapter 4

1. A. Motyer, *The Message of Exodus* (Nottingham: Inter-Varsity Press, 2005)
pp.65–66

2. B. Johnson, *Strengthen Yourself in the Lord* (Shippensburg: Destiny Image Publishers, 2007) p.18

3. J. Ortberg, *If You Want to Walk on Water, You've Got to Get out of the Boat* (Grand Rapids: Zondervan, 2001) p.10

4. @NickyGumbel on Twitter, 12 November 2014

Chapter 5

1. www.michaeljordanquotes.org/

2. R. Moses, *The 15 Secrets of Millionaires* (San Diego: Ron Moses Publishing, 2012)
p.124

Chapter 6

1. C. Calver, *Sold Out* (London: Marshall, Morgan & Scott, 1980) p.26

2. J. Eldridge, *Wild at Heart* (Nashville, Thomas Nelson Inc., 2001) p.200

3. G. Hawthorne, R. Martin, D. Reid, *Dictionary of Paul & His Letters* (Leicester: Inter-Varsity Press, 1993) p.689

4. W. W. Wiersbe *The Wiersbe Bible Commentary* (Colorado Springs: David C. Cook, 2007) p.642

5. J. A. Motyer, *The Richness of Christ* (London: Inter-Varsity Press, 1966) p.110

6. G. Fee, *Philippians* (Leicester: Inter-Varsity Press, 1999) p.127

7. M. Duncan, *Risk Takers* (Oxford: Monarch Books, 2013) pp.60–61

8. www.unitedbiblesocieties.org/wp-content/uploads/2015/03/Two-Rows-By-the-Sea-English.pdf

9. C. S. Lewis, *Mere Christianity* (New York: HarperCollins, 2001), p.192

10. www.capuk.org/about-us/the-cap-story

11. *Cinnamon Faith Action Audit* (Cinnamon Network, May 2015) p.7

12. R. Bolton, *No Fear: Don't Let Your Fears Stand in the Way of Your Dreams* (Boston: Little, Brown & Company, 1995)

Chapter 7

1. J. P. Hyatt, *Exodus* (London: Marshall, Morgan & Scott Ltd., 1971) p.183

2. J. D. Hannah, *The Bible Knowledge Commentary* (Edited by J. F. Walvoord and R. B. Zuck) (Wheaton: Victor Books, 1985) p.135

3. Ibid.

4. P. Moore, *Moses* (Oxford: Monarch Books, 2011) p.73

5. J. D. Hannah, *The Bible Knowledge Commentary* (Edited by J. F. Walvoord and R. B. Zuck) (Wheaton: Victor Books, 1985) p.135

6. R. A. Cole, *Exodus* (Leicester: Inter-Varsity Press, 1973) p.136

7. B. M. Howard, Copyright © Mission Hills Music, www.ButterflySong.com, CCLI – 35445

8. M. Henry, *Matthew Henry's Commentary on the Whole Bible in One Volume* (London: Marshall Morgan & Scott Ltd., 1994) p.90

Chapter 8

1. R. V. G. Tasker, *John* (Leicester: Inter-Varsity Press, 1999) p.191

2. I. Randall, D. Hilborn, *One Body in Christ: The History & Significance of the Evangelical Alliance* (Carlisle: Paternoster Press, 2001) p.37

3. Ibid. p.43

4. www.baptist.org.uk/Groups/220595/Declaration_of_Principle.aspx

5. M. Frost, A. Hirsch, *The Shaping of Things to Come* (Peabody: Hendrickson Publishers, 2003) p.22

6. J. Gladwin, *Love and Liberty: Faith and Unity in a Postmodern Age* (London: Darton, Longman & Todd, 1998) p.209

7. M. Buckingham, *Now Discover Your Strengths* (London: Pocket Books, 2004) p.7

Chapter 9

1. A. Emiaghe, *Seven Women, One God* (Bloomington: AuthorHouse, 2010) p.41

2. *Premier Christianity Magazine*, London, June 2015 p.74

3. J. Stott, *The Message of Romans* (Leicester: Inter-Varsity Press, 1994) p.58

4. Ibid.

5. J. John, C. Walley, *The Life* (Milton Keynes: Authentic Lifestyle, 2003) p.9

6. M. Greene, *Fruitfulness on the Frontline* (Nottingham: Inter-Varsity Press, 2014)

7. M. Greene, *Fruitfulness on the Frontline* (Nottingham: Inter-Varsity Press, 2014) p.201

8. www.thepublicleader.com

Chapter 10

1. G. J. Wenham, *Numbers* (Leicester: Inter-Varsity Press, 1981) p.115

2. Ibid. p.120

3. Ibid. p.123

4. D. Pytches, *Come, Holy Spirit* (London: Hodder & Stoughton, 1985) pp.96–97

5. S. Guillebaud (quoting Andre Gide), *Choose Life 365* (Oxford: Monarch Books, 2014) 8 January

6. M. Duncan, *Unbelievable* (Oxford: Monarch Books, 2014) p.42

Chapter 11

1. H. Nouwen, *The Return of the Prodigal Son: A Story of Homecoming* (London: Darton, Longman & Todd Ltd., 1994) pp.41–42

2. Ibid.

3. "The Last Kodak Moment?" *The Economist* www.economist.com/node/21542796

4. D. Usborne, "The Moment it All Went Wrong for Kodak", *The Independent*, 20 January 2012

5. C. Mui, *How Kodak Failed* www.forbes.com/sites/chunkamui/2012/01/18/how-kodak-failed/

Chapter 12

1. D. Beckham, *My Side* (London: Willow, 2003) p.23
2. C. Malone, "Gay wedding cake case is half-baked", *Sunday Mirror,* 24 May 15
3. O. Hillman, *Change Agent* (Lake Mary: Charisma House, 2011) p.242
4. B. Lomenick, *The Catalyst Leader* (Nashville: Thomas Nelson Inc., 2013)
5. *Talking Jesus: Perceptions of Jesus, Christians and Evangelism in England* (Research from the Barna Group on behalf of the Church of England, Evangelical Alliance and Hope, 2015) p.15
6. Ibid. p.20
7. P. Yancey, *Prayer: Does it make any difference?* (London: Hodder & Stoughton, 2008) p.197
8. P. Greig, A. Freeman, *Punk Monk: New Monasticism & the Ancient Art of Breathing* (Ada: Baker Books, 2007) p.64
9. M. Green, *The Message of Matthew* (Leicester: Inter-Varsity Press, 2000) p.278

Chapter 13

1. G. H. Jones, *The New Century Bible Commentary: 1 and 2 Kings* (Basingstoke: Marshall, Morgan & Scott, 1984) p.385
2. K. Blanchard, P. Hodges, *Lead Like Jesus* (Nashville: Thomas Nelson Inc., 2005) p.8
3. J. A. Thompson, *Deuteronomy* (Leicester: Inter-Varsity Press, 1974) p.320
4. Ibid.

Chapter 14

1. *21st Century Evangelicals: Time for Discipleship* (London: Evangelical Alliance, 2014) p.7
3. G. Calver, *Disappointed with Jesus?* (Oxford: Monarch Books, 2010) p.16
3. Ibid.

Chapter 15

1. M. Gladwell, *The Tipping Point* (London: Little, Brown Book Group, 2002)
2. D. Field, *James* (Leicester: Crossway Books, 1998) p.24
3. *Amazing Grace* (Momentum Pictures, 2006)
4. Lyrics by Thomas Chisholm
5. www.prayers-for-special-help.com/prayer-for-hope.html